A Classroom Guide

to accompany

THE NORTON ANTHOLOGY OF LITERATURE BY WOMEN

The Tradition in English

Sandra M. Gilbert
Princeton University

Susan Gubar
Indiana University

Published simultaneously in Canada by Penguin
Books Canada Ltd., 2801 John Street, Markham,
Ontario L3R 1B4.

Printed in the United States of America.


ISBN 0-393-95394-7


W. W. Norton & Company, Inc.
500 Fifth Avenue, New York, NY 10110

W. W. Norton & Company Ltd.
37 Great Russell Street, London WC1B 3NU

1 2 3 4 5 6 7 8 9 0

# CONTENTS

PREFACE    v

1. WOMEN'S STUDIES AND FEMINIST CRITICISM    1

2. TEACHING LITERATURE BY WOMEN    15

3. GENDER AND GENRE    23
   - The Novel or Novella    23
   - Short Fiction    25
     - Fantasy    25
     - Regionalism    26
     - Comedy    27
     - The Realistic    28
     - Experimentalism    29
   - Personal Prose    30
   - Expository and Polemical Prose    32
   - Drama    34
   - Poetry    35
     - The Long Poem    36
     - The Sonnet or Sonnet-Sequence    39
     - The Narrative or Dramatic Poem    41
     - The Occasional Poem    44
     - Comic Verse    46

4. THEMES OF GENDER    49
   - The Female Life Cycle    51
     - Growing Up Female    51
     - The Family: Father-Daughter Relationships    51
     - The Family: Siblings    52
     - The Family: Mothers (Having a Mother or Matrilineage)    52
     - The Single Woman    53
     - Marriage    53
     - Motherhood (Being a Mother)    54
     - Aging    55
     - Death    55
   - Women and Sexuality    56
     - Heterosexual Eroticism    56
     - Lesbianism    57

Women and Nature      58
Women and Politics        59
   General Politics:  War and Peace,
      Oppression and Slavery        59
   Feminist Politics:  Education and
      Social Protest        60
Gender and Race      61
Women and Work      62
   Domesticity and Domestic Service      62
   Women and Economics      62
Women and Spirituality      63
Women and Madness      64
Women and Violence      65
Female Communities      66
Women on Specific Women      66
Myths of Femaleness      67
Women and Creativity      68

5. ENRICHING STANDARD SURVEY, INTRODUCTORY,
   AND PERIOD COURSES        71

6. ESSAY QUESTIONS AND RESEARCH TOPICS        78
   Interpretation of Individual Texts
         and Authors        78
   Generic Questions        82
   Thematic Questions        85
   Women's Studies Issues        89
   Male and Female Literary Traditions        93
   Additional Suggestions        99

## PREFACE

Why does the <u>Norton</u> <u>Anthology</u> <u>of</u> <u>Literature</u>
<u>by</u> <u>Women</u> appear to need a classroom guide? Can
it be that literature by women is not teachable
through ordinary classroom methodology--is not,
in other words, sufficiently complex and allusive
to allow the exercise of traditional exegetical
skills? Do female literary achievements have to
be supported and sustained by some form of special pleading? Is the construction of women's
literary history merely a compensatory activity
so that it must be accompanied by tendentious
documentation? Is the field of literature by
women one that lends itself more to political
than to intellectual purposes? Or can it be that
the problems of teaching are inevitably intensi-
fied when one encounters what T.S. Eliot, writing
in a very different context, once called "the new
(the really new) work of art"? Is it possible,
in other words, that the excavation of a heretofore neglected literary tradition may necessi-
tate the formulation of at least comparatively
new classroom strategies?

Clearly we believe that the last of these
alternatives is the most reasonable: because
many of us who teach women's literature were
never ourselves taught women's literature, we
must all familiarize ourselves with a canon of
the new that in some sense obliges us to defamil-
iarize the canon of the old, and because most of
us who teach this subject were trained in far
more limited and specialized historical or generic fields, we may now all have to encounter and
assimilate material that is far more wide-ranging
(and far more unexamined) than the "mainstream"
literature which we were taught to teach. While
the field of women's literature presents unique
challenges, however, we nevertheless think it
obvious that the complexities of female writing
sustain the exercise of traditional exegetical
skills, and that such writing does not require
special pleading or tendentious documentation.

This guide, therefore, is not organized as a
series of extended, formal readings of the poems,
stories, and novels in NALW. Instead, we have
tried to present a set of intellectual approaches, pedagogical strategies, aesthetic traditions,
and thematic threads that can help instructors
teach texts which may be entirely new to them or
which may be known but have thus far remained
largely unexamined in this newly constructed
context.

Because NALW brings together selections
which, taken in their entirety, constitute the
first historical overview of women's literary
accomplishments in English, we have begun our
classroom guide with a chapter devoted to a general consideration of the critical frameworks--
women's studies and feminist literary criticism--
that have given rise to such courses as Women and
Literature, Women Writers, Images of Women in
Literature, Introduction to Women's Studies, and
Topics in Women's Studies, all of them courses in
which this anthology could be used. Some
teachers will doubtless want to organize a term-
or year-long literature class around this book,
while others may want to use the anthology as a
text for a section devoted to literature in an
interdisciplinary women's studies course. We
will consider these different possible functions
of NALW in our second chapter, a discussion of
the special issues involved in teaching literature by women.

To help provide a concise survey of the
contours of the book, Chapter 3 of this guide
will review the material in each of the historical periods represented in NALW by organizing it
along generic lines. Within the historical
framework of the six periods represented in the
anthology (Literature of the Middle Ages and the
Renaissance, Literature of the Seventeenth and
Eighteenth Centuries, Literature of the Nineteenth Century, Turn-of-the-Century Literature,
Modernist Literature, and Contemporary Literature), we trace the development of such literary
modes as the novel, the short story, autobiography, feminist expository prose, drama, the long
poem, and the sonnet. Particularly in those
cases where a text within a particular genre may
be new to teachers, we have explored strategies
for grouping texts together as well as methods of

supplementing such groupings with additional
biographical, historical, and critical background
material.

For those instructors who wish to create
courses or units of courses that cut across chronological periods or generic traditions to address enduring literary or social questions,
Chapter 4 will discuss thematic ways of approaching the texts included in the anthology.  We
will, for example, examine issues that could
organize a series of classes devoted to women's
development of specific subjects (among others,
the female life cycle; female sexuality; women
and spirituality; gender, class, and race;  myths
of femaleness). Finally, after a consideration of
how NALW might be used as a supplement to traditional anthologies of English and/or American
literature in standard introductory survey courses, our guide will conclude with a list of
possible essay and research topics that should
allow each student to use the book as a starting
point for her or his own cultural investigations.

We hope this guide will be taken in the
spirit in which it was written:  not as a set of
injunctions formulated by experts but as a series
of ideas proposed by colleagues who look forward
to experimenting with syllabi, handouts, and
reserve lists, as we--like you--begin creating
the courses that could not be taught until NALW
existed.  Indeed, because that common project is
ahead of us all, we hope you will send your own
pedagogical proposals to us (in care of W.W.
Norton, 500 Fifth Avenue, New York, NY 10110) so
we can benefit from such additional suggestions.

## WOMEN'S STUDIES AND FEMINIST CRITICISM

The theoretical rationale for studying women's literature as a coherent field has been supplied by feminist literary critics who have drawn on the wider methodological and pedagogic practices of the women's studies programs that have sprung up during the past decade in the universities of nearly every English-speaking country. To be sure, as <u>NALW</u> itself demonstrates, literary women from Margaret Cavendish and Mary Wollstonecraft to Olive Schreiner, Virginia Woolf, and Adrienne Rich have always been aware of their special situation in patriarchal culture. But--as we explain in our introduction to the <u>NALW</u> section on contemporary literature--the institutionalization of women's studies, which grew out of the sixties women's movement, made possible for the first time the development of new curricula based on a proliferating body of innovative research. While we do not have space here to offer more than a brief review of representative examples of women's studies scholarship in the humanities, we will try at least to trace four crucial strategies through which such curricula evolved: <u>critique</u>, <u>recovery</u>, <u>reconceptualization</u>, and <u>reassessment</u>. Although these strategies developed in roughly chronological order, none has obviated or replaced any other, and in fact all four continue to be effective intellectual approaches for women's studies scholars.

Women's studies research was first formulated as a <u>critique</u> of existing courses and scholarship, for women in the academy became aware in the late sixties that the arts and sciences, which were represented as universal fields of inquiry, were generally centered on exclusively male (privileged and white) subjects and points of view. Two anthologies of feminist writing--Robin Morgan's <u>Sisterhood Is Powerful</u> (1970) and Vivian Gornick's and Barbara K. Moran's <u>Woman in a Sexist Society</u> (1971)--illuminate the assumptions that would inform the growth of women's studies programs in the humanities. First, in essays that focused on--among other topics--prostitution, art history, the role of women in the Catholic Church, and theories of female sexuality, both books established the interdisciplinary nature of their enterprise. Second, as efforts to describe and explain the inequality between the sexes, both anthologies questioned the identification of cultural subordination with biological determinism, and they thereby disentangled gender from sex, role from body, destiny from anatomy. Third, Morgan and Gornick included creative work along with critical studies in their texts, in an effort to demonstrate how, in a key phrase of the day, "the personal is the political." Public and intellectual issues, these writers agreed, were inextricably related to private, emotional questions.

Finally--and perhaps most crucially--the contributors to <u>Sisterhood Is Powerful</u> and <u>Woman in a Sexist Society</u> examined the ways in which their own academic training had, in fact, reinforced cultural constructions of the female. Writing as a historian or a psychologist or an anthropologist, each had to come to terms with the fact that her own field of specialization had somehow defined woman so as to deny her full humanity. Ultimately, then, women's studies programs developed out of a need to revise humanistic inquiry so as to change an academy whose priorities reflected widespread but hitherto largely invisible assumptions of male superiority. Documenting the exclusion of women's experience from the classroom and from serious investigation, women's studies scholars began to uncover the unstated but nevertheless powerful assumption that "important" or "crucial" areas of study were generally associated with events or experiences shared only by men.

This examination of the masculine bias of education was quickly followed by numerous and still ongoing efforts to compensate for women's erasure from the past, efforts, in other words, of <u>recovery</u>. A shift in focus, for instance, freed historians to explore such female experiences as maternity, childcare, contraception, housework, the effects of war on women's employment, and the intellectual record of the women's movement. The pioneering work of Gerda Lerner, Ann Oakley, Carroll Smith Rosenberg, Bernice Carroll, Renate Bridenthal, Nancy Cott,

Eleanor Flexner, and Linda Gordon, among others, proved that social historians could begin to redress the ways in which women had been Hidden from History (1973), to quote the title of an important book by the British scholar Sheila Rowbotham.  Essential documents for the study of a frequently neglected female past were assembled in such collections as Theodore and Betty Roszak's Masculine/Feminine: Readings in Sexual Mythology and the Liberation of Women (1969), Miriam Schneir's Feminism: The Essential Documents (1972), Gerda Lerner's Black Women in White America (1972), and Nancy Cott's Root of Bitterness (1972), while earlier histories of women like Emily Jane Putnam's The Lady (1910), Ray Strachey's The Cause (1928), Winifred Holtby's Women in a Changing Civilization (1935), and Mary Beard's Woman as a Force in History (1946) were revived and reexamined.

As in history, in religious studies, art history, and psychology the attack on traditionally established categories and procedures of analysis quickly led to a revisionary focus on women.  Mary Daly's first book, The Church and the Second Sex (1968), critiqued the simultaneous idealization and humiliation of women in Catholic history, myth, and theology, while her second volume, Beyond God the Father (1973), sought a new form of divinity or transcendence through a movement of recovery, namely, through the consecration of women and their revolution. Similarly, the art historian Linda Nochlin's essay "Why Are There No Great Women Artists?," an examination of the patriarchal imperatives implicit in apparently neutral (i.e., gender-free) aesthetic institutions, preceded a series of recuperative works by, for instance, Eleanor Tufts (Our Hidden Heritage, 1974), J.J. Wilson and Karen Peterson (Women Artists, 1976), Nochlin and Ann Sutherland Harris (Women Artists, 1550-1950, 1976), and Germaine Greer (The Obstacle Race, 1979)--all books devoted to the art produced by women.  Similarly, women in psychology began their revisionary enterprise with Shulamith Firestone's, Jean Miller Baker's, Naomi Weisstein's, and Phyllis Chesler's different but equally intense expressions of concern about the ways in which the phallic assumptions of Sigmund Freud and other hegemonic theorists of personal-

ity appeared to turn woman into what Germaine
Greer called _The Female Eunuch_ (1971).  However,
such work was soon followed by research in the
mode of Juliet Mitchell's _Feminism and Psycho-
analysis_ (1975), studies which emphasized a specifically female perspective on human psychology;
Mitchell, for instance, revised Freud's concept
of "penis envy" by viewing it as an accurate
description of how women's cultural powerlessness
is anatomically symbolized in patriarchal society.  These women's studies scholars did not and
indeed do not adhere to any single methodology.
Yet, whether Marxists, Freudians, phenomenolo-
gists, or structuralists, they sought and seek to
recover what the poet Carolyn Kizer has called
"the world's best kept secret: / Merely the private lives of one-half of humanity."

As scholars moved from critique to the crea-
tion of alternative perspectives and fields of
inquiry, however, it became clear that traditional categories of analysis would have to be
_reconceptualized_.  In particular, a number of
theorists in anthropology and psychology were
beginning to demonstrate that feminist attention
to gender might furnish explanations for the
nature of human culture that were at least as
powerful as the class-centered Marxist notions of
property and production. In an important essay
entitled "Is Female to Male as Nature Is to
Culture?" (1974), Sherry B. Ortner traced what
she claimed were virtually universal associations
of the male with culture, associations that rele-
gated woman to a less than human status.  A few
years later, Dorothy Dinnerstein's _The Mermaid
and the Minotaur_ (1976) argued that a general
cultural malaise could be attributed to sexual
arrangements based on dread and hatred of women,
suggesting that misogyny is born of the fact
that, because women do the primary parenting in
most societies, they are inevitably perceived by
both sons and daughters as powerful, hence fear-
ful.  Working with the same given, the psychologist Nancy Chodorow asserted in _The Reproduction
of Mothering_ (1978) that both men and women were
inexorably marked by their different pre-Oedipal
relationships with the mother: because masculinity is based on differentiation from the female
parent, while femininity is based on reciprocity
and interidentification between mother and

daughter, she speculated that men's identities
are more fragile and bounded, less emotionally
receptive, than women's.  Developing a similarly
revisionary mode of analysis, in Rayna R. Rei-
ter's anthology Toward an Anthropology of Women
(1975) the scholar Gayle Rubin integrated the
sociocultural theories of Claude Levi-Strauss,
the psychoanalytic hypotheses of Sigmund Freud
and Jacques Lacan, and the socioeconomic ideas of
Karl Marx to produce in "The Traffic in Women" a
female-centered account of the relationship between gender, personality, and society.
     The construction of such new conceptual
models for understanding women's experience involved a recognition that--despite the usefulness
of, say, Freud or Levi-Strauss to theoreticians
like Chodorow and Rubin--many intellectual paradigms provided by traditional scholars required
reassessment.  For instance, a  landmark essay by
Joan Kelly, entitled "The Social Relation of the
Sexes:  Methodological Implications of Women's
History" (Signs, 1976), demonstrated that the
usual models of historical periodization could
not be used to represent women's past.  Indeed,
Kelly observed, because women's history does not
"fit into" received periods, that history calls
into question most conventional attempts at historical periodization.  More recently, Carol
Gilligan has questioned the monolithic model of
ethical development presented by the psychologist
Lawrence Kohlberg.  Her In a Different Voice
(1982) argues that women, who are described as
"immature" or "irresponsible" when measured by
Kohlberg's criteria, can be considered nurturing
and supportive when viewed from a female-centered
ethical perspective.  Thus, by placing male and
female models side by side, both Kelly and Gilligan have revealed the way in which issues raised
by women's studies might radically alter the
considerations and conclusions of traditional
scholarship.  Following their lead, scholars in
many other fields are now working toward a reassessment of culture that would place the experiences of men and women in a context which
includes the history of gender arrangements and
their impact on all modes of human endeavor.
     Not surprisingly, feminist literary criti-
cism has evolved through phases that parallel
those through which women's studies grew:  it,

too, followed a pattern of critique, recovery,
reconceptualization, and reassessment. Indeed,
it is arguable that feminist literary critics
were often pioneers in developing such strategies.  To begin with, scholars of English and
American literature turned their attention to the
stereotypical presentations of women in male-
created literature.  Basing their investigations
on Simone de Beauvoir's analysis of woman as the
other (in The Second Sex, 1949), these critics
uncovered the sex bias behind such images of
women as the bitch, the sex goddess, the old
maid, the mammy, the neurotic or inept poetess,
the angel in the house, and the castrating
mother.  Focusing on misogynistic descriptions of
women and oppressive prescriptions for women,
Katherine Rogers (in The Troublesome Helpmate,
1966), Mary Ellmann (in Thinking about Women,
1968), and Kate Millett (in Sexual Politics,
1971) explored the elevation and devaluation of
female characters depicted only in terms of masculine desire and dread.  Antithetically, Carolyn
Heilbrun envisioned escape from the bind and
binary of gender through the subversive imaginings of androgyny that she saw as a hidden theme
in literary history (Toward a Recognition of
Androgyny, 1973).  At the same time, books like
Susan Koppelman Cornillon's anthology of critical
essays, Images of Women in Fiction (1972), and
Judith Fryer's analysis of American literature,
The Faces of Eve (1976), accepted the position,
articulated by Millett, that criticism must take
into account "the larger cultural context in
which literature is conceived and produced."
Such critiques, which have drawn attention to the
sometimes disturbing uses male writers have made
of women, are still far from complete.  Rogers'
book, for example, has been followed by histories of misogyny in specific literary periods
(like Felicity Nussbaum's The Brink of All We
Hate [1984] on the Restoration and early
eighteenth century), while such books as Annette
Kolodny's The Lay of the Land (1976)--on American
literature--explore the sexual dynamics of the
metaphors male writers use to construct a vision
of their world that exploits femaleness while
relegating real women to the margins of experience.
        Kolodny's next book--The Land Before Her:

<u>Fantasies</u> <u>and</u> <u>Experiences</u> <u>of</u> <u>the</u> <u>American</u> <u>Fron-</u>
<u>tiers, 1630-1860</u> (1984)--typifies the shift of
feminist criticism from <u>critique</u> to <u>recovery</u>, for
in it she examines the neglected journals and
letters of female pioneers whose language reveals
a quite different response to the New World than
that of their male contemporaries.  What Elaine
Showalter has called "gynocriticism" began in
1975 and 1976 with the publication of Patricia
Meyer Spacks' <u>The</u> <u>Female</u> <u>Imagination</u> and Ellen
Moers' <u>Literary</u> <u>Women</u>.  (In its way, Elizabeth
Hardwick's <u>Seduction</u> <u>and</u> <u>Betrayal:</u> <u>Women</u> <u>and</u>
<u>Literature</u> [1970] might also be said to move
toward this critical mode, because it combines
analyses of male images of women with considerations of women's depictions of themselves.)
Quickly followed by Showalter's <u>A</u> <u>Literature</u> <u>of</u>
<u>Their</u> <u>Own</u> (1977) and by our own <u>The</u> <u>Madwoman</u> <u>in</u>
<u>the</u> <u>Attic</u> (1979), these "gynocritical" texts
attempted to locate the common themes, images,
and literary strategies employed by women writers.
     Whether the source of such commonality was
thought to lie in anatomical distinctions between
the sexes, in women's exclusion from mainstream
literary conventions, or in a women's subculture
analagous to a colonized subculture, the fact of
female literary commonality seemed to some critics to demonstrate the existence of an alternative literary history that placed already established texts in new contexts even as it consti-
tuted a tradition in which readers could place
works of art that had mistakenly been consigned
to oblivion.  In some books--notably Suzanne
Juhasz's <u>Naked</u> <u>and</u> <u>Fiery</u> <u>Forms</u> (1976), Emily
Stipes Watts' <u>The</u> <u>Poetry</u> <u>of</u> <u>American</u> <u>Women</u> <u>from</u>
<u>1632</u> <u>to</u> <u>1945</u> (1977), our own <u>Shakespeare's</u> <u>Sis-</u>
<u>ters</u> (1979), Margaret Homans' <u>Women</u> <u>and</u> <u>Poetic</u>
<u>Identity</u> (1980), and Cheryl Walker's <u>The</u> <u>Nightin-</u>
<u>gale's</u> <u>Burden</u> (1982)--poetry emerged as a special
theoretical problem for women writers.  At the
same time, the great tradition of nineteenth-
century fiction was approached from widely different perspectives in a number of other works,
including Ann Douglas's <u>The</u> <u>Feminization</u> <u>of</u>
<u>American</u> <u>Culture</u> (1977), Nina Auerbach's <u>Communi-</u>
<u>ties</u> <u>of</u> <u>Women</u> (1978) and <u>Woman</u> <u>and</u> <u>the</u> <u>Demon</u>
(1983), and Nina Baym's <u>Woman's</u> <u>Fiction</u> (1978).
     As diverse as they were, many of these

studies involved scholars in <u>reconceptualizing</u>
literary history.  Specifically, by excavating
popular forms that had previously been dismissed
as irrelevant, such feminist scholars fostered
questions about our inherited notions of the past
as well as about the criteria by which our notions of literary excellence are formed.  Soci-
ologists of culture, for instance, began to study
the economic and ideological implications of the
literary marketplace in order to examine the
differing status of some significant male-  and
female-authored classics, trying to explain why,
say, <u>Huckleberry Finn</u> had produced a veritable
Mark Twain industry, while <u>The Awakening</u> had left
Kate Chopin without either a standard edition or
a definitive, scholarly biography until Per Sey-
ersted's <u>Kate Chopin</u> appeared in 1969.  In addition, the reissuing of such texts as Charlotte
Perkins Gilman's "The Yellow Wallpaper," Rebecca
Harding Davis's <u>Life in the Iron-Mills</u>, Zora
Neale Hurston's <u>Their Eyes Were Watching God</u>, and
May Sinclair's <u>Mary Oliver</u> led to similar revisions of the canon and of those principles of
evaluation which appear to determine the "great-
ness" of supposedly classic texts.

At the same time, critics of black, working-
class, and lesbian literature responded to the
erasure of those traditions by recovering works
which could now be freshly historicized; for
example, Gloria Hull, Erlene Stetson, and Mary
Helen Washington edited and analyzed texts written by black women, while Florence Howe and Tillie Olsen focused on the achievements of working-
class women writers, and Blanche W. Cook, Lillian
Faderman, and Bonnie Zimmerman explored the work
of lesbian authors.  Such projects, we should
stress, were and are part of an enterprise that
is still ongoing.  Recently, some critics--for
instance, Paula Gunn Allen, Dexter Fisher, and
Rayne Green--have begun to analyze and antholo-
gize the writings of native-American women, while
others--for instance, Marcela Christine Lucero-
Trujillo and Tey Diane Rebolledo--have started to
study the rapidly evolving Chicana and Latina
literary tradition, a tradition that (though
often bilingual) has become increasingly visible
in the United States since the 1960s.  Similarly,
Helen Barolini has just produced a collection of
contemporary texts by Italian-American women, and

such critics as Sonya Michel, Erika Duncan, and
Esther Cohen have lately begun to excavate and
investigate the literary tradition pioneered by
Jewish-American women.  Finally, a number of
writers and editors--among them, Fay Chiang, Emma
Gee, and Janice Mirikitani--have assembled and
published works by Asian-Americans.  An extremely
useful overview of a number of these complex and
quickly·growing bodies of writing was presented
in Dexter Fisher's anthology The Third Woman
(1980), but there is clearly a great deal more
work to be done in the field.

Besides disrupting any complacence teachers
of literature might have had about their compe-
tence to deal with a closed set of certifiably
classic texts, such an opening up of the canon
led to the structuring of new courses and to the
production of much new scholarship on such un-
canonized forms of popular literature as the
romance and on heretofore trivialized genres like
letters or memoirs.  Neglected artists--Mary
Astell, Rebecca Cox Jackson, Anna Wickham, and
Meridel Le Sueur, among others--are only now
beginning to be studied in essays and biographies.  Just as important, already established
writers--for example, Emily Dickinson and Virginia Woolf--are now being read in light of their
relationship to a newly defined female tradition.
As feminist literary critics call for a reevalu-
ation of male-authored literature and male-con-
structed literary history, moreover, they are
drawing on a body of theoretical writing on the
subject of creativity and gender, theory that
reassesses many commonly received notions about
the production and reception of literature.

Once an understanding of creativity began to
be filtered through the lens of gender, basic
ideas about the author, the text, and the reader
began to receive attention from feminist theorists of literature.  About the author, for instance, we ourselves have argued in The Madwoman
that in patriarchal culture theological, political, and aesthetic authority accrues to the male
so that creativity is profoundly associated with
masculinity.  The woman author, who experiences
herself as a contradiction in terms, confronts a
double bind that Virginia Woolf described some
six decades ago:  either she writes like a man or
she is nothing but a second-rate "feminine" wri-

ter.  Thus, while male artists may confront the
"anxiety of influence" that the critic Harold
Bloom identifies with a fear of belatedness in a
tradition that stretches back to Milton and
Shakespeare, women writers confront a prior and
even more debilitating anxiety of authorship, a
dread that they cannot create without isolating
themselves from other women and from the female
in themselves.

For those women artists who managed to evade
the silences that the critic-novelist Tillie
Olsen has documented in several important essays,
we have claimed that creativity seems to involve
a splitting of the self, a fragmentation which is
reflected in the narrative and metaphorical doubling that haunts literature produced by women,
artists who often associate their own creativity
with rebellion, anger, or even monstrosity.  Because of this anxiety, too, women writers--as a
number of theorists besides us have argued--tend
to look to each other for some assurance that
they need not think of themselves as "singular
anomalies."  From Ellen Moers to Susan Friedman,
feminist critics have documented the ties between, say, Elizabeth Barrett Browning and Emily
Dickinson or between H.D. and Adrienne Rich.  The
dynamics of influence, such scholars imply, may
be less agonistic for women writers than for male
authors.

That the themes of women's letters are
shaped by the experiences of women's lives and
specifically by women's roles as mothers,
daughters, wives, lovers, and sisters is, of
course, obvious.  In addition, given the explos-
ively rebellious stance of the woman artist who
defies the silence, self-abnegation, and docility
fostered by feminine socialization, it is hardly
surprising that women's literature frequently
makes use of spatial imagery, moving between
nightmares of a dreaded domestic confinement and
dreams of having "a room of one's own."  But
feminist literary critics have also lately demonstrated that women write from a special perspective and with particular intensity about the
female body (anorexia, agoraphobia, white-defined
standards of beauty, reproduction, rape), about
the female community (female friendships, lesbianism), about family dynamics (father-daughter
relationships, mother-daughter ties, sibling ri-

valries), and about the dynamics of female creativity (the gender of the woman writer's "muse").
At the same time, moreover, besides suggesting
that women writers share specific subjects, a
number of critics--including ourselves--have argued that the woman's text presents itself as a
palimpsest, a decorous surface which often hides
an encoded, subversive subtext.  Working respec-
tively with French novels, American short stories, and lesbian poetry and prose, for example,
Nancy Miller, Annette Kolodny, and Catharine
Stimpson have recently published essays that
disclose encoded subtexts hidden behind or sub-
merged beneath apparently conventional scripts.

While feminist critics have considered the
relationship between textuality and sexuality,
feminist linguists have analyzed women's ambiva-
lent attitude toward language.  Specifically,
many feminist theorists have argued that women's
alienation from patriarchal culture implies the
possibility that women have a relationship to
language different from that of men. In America,
England, and France, two schools of thinkers have
begun to analyze syntax, vocabulary, and--
indeed--the very notion of language itself in
order to illuminate the relationship between
gender and "the symbolic order."  From Robin
Lakoff (Language and Woman's Place, 1975), Mary
Hiatt (The Way Women Write, 1977), and Casey
Miller and Kate Smith (Words and Women, 1977) to
Dale Spender (Man Made Language, 1980), Sally
McConnell Ginet, Ruth Borker, and Nelly Furman
(Women and Language, Literature and Society,
1980), and Cheris Kramerae (Women and Men
Speaking, 1981), Anglo-American empiricists  have
documented the ways in which women are perceived
to employ a language less forceful than that of
men.  Focusing for the most part (with the excep-
tion of Hiatt) on spoken language, they have
analyzed lexical asymmetries ("poet," "poetess"),
patterns of interruption frequency (female speakers are more often interrupted than male speakers), and syntactic structures (women employ a
preponderance of hedging or interrogative forms)
to document the devaluation of women and women's
language.

In France, a more theoretical investigation
of female discourse by such thinkers as Julia
Kristeva, Hélène Cixous, and Luce Irigaray has

produced an often lyrical exploration of the ways
in which the "dark continent" of "the feminine"
might be inscribed into a discourse dominated by
and created out of "phallologocentrism."  For
these thinkers, the binary opposition of culture
and nature, man and woman, reflects the hierarchy
of the signifier (the word) and the signified
(the thing).  With woman a silent object signified by male discourse, they argue, she must
speak (when she speaks as woman) a language of
the body that disrupts and subverts the patriarchal order.

Whether it is shaped by Anglo-American em-
piricism or colored by the more abstract cast of
French theory, such linguistic thinking has generated much controversy on both sides of the
Atlantic.  Nevertheless, whether one supports,
say, Lakoff or Cixous--or neither--one must
concede that their work calls attention to the
radicalism of the feminist intellectual project,
a project that questions and thereby reassesses
even the neutrality of the supposedly "neutral"
phenomenon of language.  Clearly, for women artists, whose very adoption of a name is often
problematic, both speaking and writing are in
some sense gender-marked processes.

Reading, too, as many feminist critics have
suggested, is such a process.  Most notably perhaps, Judith Fetterley has developed the idea of
a "resisting reader," a woman who sheds aesthetic
responses learned through a kind of male mimicry
to enter texts from a specifically female position.  For Fetterley, whose The Resisting Reader
(1975) traced the ways in which classic American
prose narratives from Washington Irving's short
story "Rip Van Winkle" to F. Scott Fitzgerald's
novel The Great Gatsby valorize male experience
and thus require the woman reader to "identify
against herself," "the major works of American
fiction constitute a series of designs on the
female reader, all the more potent in their
effect because they are 'impalpable.'" To refuse
to merge one's reading mind with male experience
is to uncover those designs and recover a self
that is no longer defined as merely "not male."
While Fetterley and, more recently, Jonathan
Culler in his "Reading as a Woman" (On Decon-
struction, 1983) focus on the female reader of
male-authored texts, a number of reader-response

critics like Jane Tompkins, Susan Suleiman, Norman Holland, and David Bleich have begun to explore the reading process either by empirically
documenting the different reactions of male and
female readers or by speculating on what literature itself tells us about the relationship between socialization and reading.  At the same
time, approaching the issue from a somewhat different perspective, such psychoanalytic critics
as Elizabeth Abel, Claire Kahane, and Judith
Kegan Gardiner have begun to use object-relations
theory to explain what they view as the especially intense identification of women readers with
female characters.  Finally, a number of books by
such feminist critics as Susan Griffin, Laura
Lederer, and Andrea Dworkin have examined the
psychological and ethical effects of pornography
on both male and female readers, studying in
particular the relationship between reading and
sexual violence.

     None of the critics reviewed here would, of
course, deny the diversity of women's lives and
letters:  race and class, as well as historical
and geographical factors, clearly distinguish
women writers (and readers) from each other.  Nor
would these critics imply that the study of traditional male literary history can simply be
replaced by the examination of a newly visible
female tradition.  On the contrary, as Myra Jeh-
len proposed in "Archimedes and the Paradox of
Feminist Criticism" (_Signs_, 1981), a number of
feminist literary historians are now calling for
a map of reading that charts not only the inter-
personal dynamics of male and female pairs of
artists (for instance, Elizabeth Barrett Browning
and Robert Browning, Edith Wharton and Henry
James, or Sylvia Plath and Ted Hughes), but also
the interactional strategies of male- and female-
identified traditions, conventions, and genres.
But this work could not be done until the female
tradition emerged from critical eclipse. Even
more important, such a project could not be
undertaken until the vitality and variety of
women's literary inheritance were fully established.  Whether **NALW** is used specifically to
explore women's literary accomplishments, whether
it functions as one component of an investigation
into women's cultural history, or whether it is
employed to enrich our understanding of literary

history in general, we hope it will help place
female creativity at the center of critical discourse.    After all, who knows how the male literary tradition will look when it is perceived as a
supplement to "herstory?"

# 2

# TEACHING LITERATURE BY WOMEN

Some teachers consider the study of women's literature a short-term antidote to long-term neglect while others see such study as a crucially transformative solution to oppression; in other words, some believe that the female literary canon must eventually be "mainstreamed"-- assimilated into a more general canon of English and American literature--while others hold that women's literature must and should continue indefinitely to be studied as a subject in its own right. Whatever their assumptions are in this regard, however, teachers of literature by women inevitably discover that they are working in a classroom climate quite different from that of more conventional courses. In essays, lectures, and conference talks, as well as on course evaluation forms, students and teachers alike have expressed surprise at their own excited responses to discussions sparked by women's literature.

Some of the reasons for this excitement are obvious. More than many other disciplines, women's studies in general and women's literature in particular are linked to issues and people outside the academy, both through the public political goals of the women's movement and through the personal goals of individual women in a period of sociocultural transition. Given the intensity generated by such goals, it is not surprising that both female and male readers often tend to respond with personal fervor to texts that frequently seem (especially to women students) to deal quite specifically with problems that they have themselves confronted in their own lives.

Although such intensity often transforms the women's literature classroom into a uniquely volcanic arena--a site, sometimes, of discussions that sound more like encounter groups or "consciousness-raising" activities than modes of academic discourse--there are a number of reasons why teachers of women's literature might want actively to encourage subjective responses from their students. Some instructors believe, for

instance, that genuine intellectual insight is
frequently achieved through or accompanied by
personal interactions and changes.  Just as important, because feminist historians like Barbara
Ehrenreich and Deirdre English (_For Her Own Good:
150 Years of the Experts' Advice to Women_, 1978)
have suggestively explored a number of ways in
which women have frequently been victimized or
ignored by academic and medical professionals and
specialists, many teachers want to encourage
female students to question the authority that
women are generally socialized to accept both in
and out of the classroom.

In other words, because women have been
spoken or written about more than they have spoken or written for themselves, many teachers see
the women's literature classroom as a place to
address and redress a historic imbalance.  Some
see that classroom, too, as a place in which
teacher and students alike can begin to uncover,
in the words of Bari Watkins, director of the
Program on Women at Northwestern University, the
ways in which "our earliest notions of human
culture were in fact ideological justifications
of a particular distribution of power within society."  She and others like her believe, therefore, that within the classroom itself, students
who are being asked to examine the ideological
assumptions behind authoritative cultural structures ought to be made aware of the politics of
pedagogy.

Historically excluded from such politics,
teachers of women's studies and feminist criticism often agree with Virginia Woolf that, although it is "unpleasant" to be shut out, "it is
worse perhaps to be locked in."  Rather than
replicate the solipsistic stance of Professor Von
X in _A Room of One's Own_ or the self-certifying
processions of professional men in _Three Guineas_,
such instructors attempt to decentralize the
traditional classroom in order to suggest an
alternative educational model, one based less on
superiority than on mutuality.  After all,
women's literature, like feminist criticism, is
centrally concerned with the dynamics of domi-
nance, and thus many teachers put into question
pedagogic authority, along with such traditional
academic goals as "objectivity," "universality,"
"expertise," and "impartiality." Similarly, many

reject such academic pieties as the traditional
separation of disciplines, the individualistic
enterprise of scholarship, and the hierarchical
relationship between theory and practice--the
last of which Mary Daly has sardonically termed
"the tyranny of methodolotry."

As worthy as the revisionary educational
project of women's studies is, however, it can
generate its own set of problems.  Class discussions can get scattered or grow so personal that
some students become embarrassed, bored, or
alienated.  Before they analyze the complexity of
a literary text, moreover, some students--those
who are apt to identify with the heroines of
women's literature--may search for "positive role
models" and, as the teacher of Kate Chopin and
Sylvia Plath often discovers, they can become
extremely depressed at not finding them.  More
problematic still, those students who replace
aesthetic standards of evaluation with ideological criteria may reject writing that does not
conform to their definition of feminism or they
may attempt to endow such writing with a contemporary political perspective.  In addition, because teachers do know more about the dynamics of
literary texts than their students do, well-
meaning instructors may create an atmosphere of
bad faith, asking questions that only they can
answer.  Just as important, regardless of instructors' efforts to question or qualify their
own authority, the grades they must give clearly
imply an inexorable authority, even when self-
grading procedures are used.

Worse still, teachers who avoid presenting a
personal reading of a text as a definitive one
nevertheless often experience feelings of inade-
quacy:  after all, they are not likely to be
familiar with up-to-date scholarship in all of
the disciplines that converge on the interpretation of women's literature, and, yet more problematic, they may never even have studied women's
literature in graduate school, for the simple
reason that courses in the subject did not exist
until little more than a decade ago.  (Further-
more, instructors cannot always find scholarly
help in the library: some of the early periods in
women's literary history have not yet been fully
explored, and a number of newly recovered texts
have not yet been subjected to the sort of anal-

yses teachers can expect to find for works in the
standard canon.)
    Finally, besides the problems sometimes
posed by class and room size, matters frequently
not in the instructor's control, many teachers
and students in women's literature courses may
face complex group dynamics because of the implicitly political nature of the women's studies
enterprise.  If a class is all-female, there may
be unspoken rifts between blacks and whites or
between lesbians and heterosexuals.  If it is
coeducational, some men and women may feel inhib-
ited from expressing themselves fully and honest-
ly.  If it is interdisciplinary, there may be
striking differences in the lexical sophistica-
tion and methodological approaches of different
students.
    There are no simple solutions to this range
of problems, but each difficulty presents a po-
tential opportunity for an intellectual endeavor
that is exciting because ongoing.  While teaching
together or separately, we have tried a number of
techniques which have seemed to address such
issues with some success.  We offer them with
trepidation, remembering (as we always do) those
sessions in which they did not work.
    One strategy which has almost always been
effective for us in both women's literature
classes and women's studies courses is' the
assignment of journal-writing:  we ask students
to keep journals in which they regularly record
responses to the reading we are doing in class.
They are therefore free to define the nature and
level of their reactions to women's words in
spontaneous, personal language. Checked but not
graded, journals have gained us insight into
those aspects of student thinking that not all
class members may want to communicate in public.
    What work for us, too, are fairly open-ended
discussions, in which students sometimes define
the issues to be explored, along with brief lectures, where necessary information can be quickly
communicated.  Like many other instructors, we
have experimented with several discussion for-
mats:  breaking students into small groups that
analyze different characters in a single novel or
different approaches to a specific poem, and then
asking each group to "report back to" or lead a
discussion of the whole class;  going around the

room, with everyone seated in a circle, to ask
for reactions to a particularly challenging or
exciting text;  asking students to sign up at the
beginning of the semester for brief "position
papers" outlining one or two crucial ideas about
an author or work (these are Xeroxed for the
whole class and usually elicit general discussion).  In addition, of course, we simply begin
many conversations ourselves, by asking a series
of interrelated and increasingly complex questions.  As for lecturing, we reserve that proce-
dure to introduce material students cannot be
expected easily to learn on their own.  Even in
this situation, however, background information
can be made available (at least in smaller-sized
classes) so students can form their own opinions
about it.  When beginning to work on a particular
genre or historical period, we have frequently
distributed mimeographed handouts:  samples of
theological documents, quotations from medical
texts, excerpts from conduct books, passages from
pertinent male-authored literature, and even
selective historical chronologies.

As most teachers are well aware, it is difficult in undergraduate literature courses to
assess students' prior knowledge of traditional
literary history.  When teaching Margery Kempe,
for example, it would probably not be safe to
assume that students are familiar with the significance of the spiritual pilgrimage in the literature of the Middle Ages.  Similarly, teachers
might be unsure about how to present the poetry
of Anne Finch without some consideration of Alexander Pope.  Again, how can <u>Jane</u> <u>Eyre</u>'s brooding
characters be understood without some analysis of
Byron's influence on Charlotte Brontë?  In our
general introductions to each period and in our
headnotes, we have tried to furnish in <u>NALW</u> some
background points about "mainstream" literary
history.  But each teacher can work up additional
background lectures, handouts, or reserve-room
reading lists so that, say, Margaret Fuller's
thought can come into focus in the context of
American Transcendentalism.  Similarly, slide
presentations of Pre-Raphaelite paintings might
illuminate either the poetry of Christina Rossetti or a general examination of the image of
the <u>femme</u> <u>fatale</u> in late nineteenth-century literature.  Finally, students themselves can help

their peers by giving oral reports on either
"mainstream" literary history or women's social
history. The medieval convent, Renaissance court-
ly love rhetoric, eighteenth-century ad feminam
satires, the role of the governess or the prosti-
tute in Victorian England, suffragist activism--
any one of these subjects could be assigned as a
research topic for a class presentation.

Teachers of literature courses may also, of
course, wish to supplement the material in NALW
with other readings. Depending on the length and
focus of a course, it might make sense to include
in the syllabus more than the three novels we
have reprinted: Jane Austen's Northanger Abbey or
Persuasion, Mary Shelley's Frankenstein, Emily
Brontë's Wuthering Heights, George Eliot's The
Mill on the Floss, Sarah Orne Jewett's The Country of the Pointed Firs, Edith Wharton's The
House of Mirth or Summer, Virginia Woolf's Mrs.
Dalloway or To the Lighthouse, and Zora Neale
Hurston's Their Eyes Were Watching God--all would
be likely candidates for use as supplementary
texts. As with novels, so with plays:  besides
works by the female playwrights of the Restoration period (Aphra Behn or Susannah Centlivre),
plays by such writers as Lorraine Hansberry,
Lillian Hellman, Adrienne Kennedy, Megan Terry,
Marsha Norman, and Caryl Churchill might be read,
viewed, or acted out in conjunction with selections in NALW.

In addition, some teachers might want to
supplement our selections with assignments of
extra material by writers working in several
genres or by teaching a complete text where we
were obliged to excerpt. Our selections from
Fanny Burney's Diary might be enriched by her
novel Evelina; Charlotte Perkins Gilman's "The
Yellow Wallpaper" might be illuminated by her
utopian fiction Herland or her polemical book
Women and Economics; Elizabeth Bishop's poems
might be complemented by her short stories "In
the Village" and "Gwendolyn." Similarly, instructors emphasizing, say, the Victorian period could
ask students to buy paperback editions of Elizabeth Barrett Browning's Aurora Leigh, Elizabeth
Gaskell's Cranford, or Linda Brent's Incidents in
the Life of a Slave Girl, so that they could read
these texts in their entirety. Finally, some
teachers might want to assign outside reading in

the oeuvres of such writers as Mary Manley, Eliza
Haywood, Lydia Maria Child, Elizabeth Stuart
Phelps Ward, Fanny Fern, Hannah More, Mary Eliza-
beth Braddon, George Egerton, Anne Spencer, Vita
Sackville-West, Mina Loy, Christina Stead, Har-
riet Arnow, Jane Bowles, Caroline Gordon, Jean
Stafford, Tess Slesinger, Naomi Replansky, June
Jordan, Olga Broumas, Sandra McPherson, Jori
Graham, Amy Clampitt, Ai, Mari Evans, Paula Gunn
Allen, Joan Didion, Diane Johnson, Diana Ó Hehir,
and many others.

For those teachers using <u>NALW</u> in a women's
studies course, there is probably no need to
assign any supplementary literature.  The anthology could be used in such a course in two quite
distinct ways.  Should the instructor wish to
focus on female creativity, a unit on women's
literature could simply be organized around the
texts the teacher finds most illuminating, pos-
sibly those works (listed in one of our thematic
tables) that focus directly on the problems creativity poses for women.  Alternatively, and perhaps more interestingly, an instructor could
integrate texts from <u>NALW</u> into each unit of the
syllabus.  Two recent publications--a textbook by
the Hunter College Women's Studies Collective
entitled <u>Women's Realities, Women's Choices</u> and
an anthology of essays entitled <u>Women: A Feminist Perspective</u> edited by Jo Freeman--indicate
the sorts of topics most introductory women's
studies courses cover.  <u>Women's Realities,
Women's Choices</u> is organized around three major
issues:  "Defining Women" (ideas about women,
their bodies, and their personalities), "The
Family Circle" (women's roles in the family,
marriage, divorce, motherhood, widowhood, alternatives to the family), and "Women in Society"
(religion, education, work, and politics).
<u>Women: A Feminist Perspective</u> addresses similar
subjects:  "The Body and Its Control," "In and
Out of the Family," "Growing Up Female," "The
Working Woman," "Institutions of Social Control,"
and "Feminism."  All these topics are central in
the female literary tradition, and all of them
are examined in the poems, stories, journals,
plays, and novels included in <u>NALW</u>.  Using the
thematic tables in Chapter 4 of this guide,
teachers could enrich contemporary essays and
articles on these subjects by assigning comparab-

ly oriented literary works from the Middle Ages
to the present.

When teaching both literature and women's
studies courses, but perhaps especially graduate
classes in both areas, it might also be profit-
able to pair specific literary texts with contemporary theoretical essays on gender. Without
privileging either literature or theory, such an
investigation could inspire original scholarly
research. An obvious strategy would be to pair a
short essay by a French feminist-linguist (for
example, Cixous's "The Laugh of the Medusa")
with texts by an experimental writer like Gertrude Stein;  to group speculations by psycholo-
gists of female development with such Bildungsro-
mans as Jane Eyre, or O'Brien's "A Rose in the
Heart";  to set essays by Marxist-feminists in
the context of prose fiction about the working
class (Life in the Iron-Mills) or political verse
by a poet like Muriel Rukeyser;  to group work by
theorists of black women's culture with The
Bluest Eye or with the poetry of Wheatley, Harper, Brooks, and Clifton;  to read recent feminist work on religion along with the writings of
mystics from Julian of Norwich to Jane Lead,
Rebecca Cox Jackson, and H.D.;  to pair Rich's
essay on "Compulsory Heterosexuality and Lesbian
Existence" (in Signs, 1980) with literature about
lesbianism by H.H. Richardson, Amy Lowell, Radclyffe Hall, and Rich herself;  to couple a classic essay in social history like Carroll Smith
Rosenberg's "The Female World of Love and Ritual:
Relations between Women in Nineteenth-Century
America" (Signs, 1975) with Jane Austen's Love
and Freindship or works by Stowe, Alcott, Jewett,
and Chopin. In all these cases, theory and literature would surely be illuminated, if not transformed, by such a dialogue, engaging students in
research that could lead either to new readings
of literary texts or to a revised perspective on
current theory.

3

## GENDER AND GENRE

As should be obvious from its table of contents, <u>NALW</u> could be used to support a straightforward historical survey of literature by women from the Middle Ages to the present. Similarly, the book could also be used as a text for a major authors course in literature by women: strong candidates for inclusion in that case would be Anne Bradstreet, Anne Finch, Mary Wollstonecraft, Jane Austen, Mary Shelley, Elizabeth Barrett Browning, Margaret Fuller, Harriet Beecher Stowe, Charlotte Brontë, Emily Brontë, George Eliot, Emily Dickinson, Christina Rossetti, Kate Chopin, Charlotte Perkins Gilman, Edith Wharton, Willa Cather, Gertrude Stein, Virginia Woolf, H.D., Marianne Moore, Zora Neale Hurston, Elizabeth Bishop, Gwendolyn Brooks, Doris Lessing, Denise Levertov, Adrienne Rich, Toni Morrison, Sylvia Plath, and Margaret Atwood.

What may be less plain from the table of contents, however, are the ways in which <u>NALW</u> might function to illuminate women's visions, versions, and revisions of by now standard literary genres. For while women have worked in most such genres, they have consistently approached and shaped conventional forms from perspectives developed by distinctively female experiences, so that genre study may well yield significant insights into the relationship between tradition and the female talent. Moreover, because of the special relationship between women and literary tradition, certain genres appear to have become especially central to female-authored literature, at least to female-authored literature in English.

## THE NOVEL OR NOVELLA

The novel is one such genre. As Virginia Woolf's remarks in <u>A Room of One's Own</u> about "the four great novelists" of the nineteenth century (Jane Austen, Charlotte Brontë, Emily Brontë, and George Eliot) along with her anxious statement that women's poetic impulses are "still denied outlet" suggest, women--even earlier women than Woolf's quartet of notables--tended to enter literary history and culture through their deployment of the supposedly lesser genre of prose fiction. Many historians of the novel, after all, would trace the inception of that form back to Aphra Behn's construction of Oroonoko (1688), and others would follow what Ian Watt has called "the rise of the novel" by describing the development of the genre in works by such female authors as Mary Manley, Eliza Haywood, Fanny Burney, Maria Edgeworth, Charlotte Smith, and Jane Austen.

Our first selection here, Jane Austen's Love and Freindship, was chosen not only for its comic charm but also because both formally and thematically it refers to and parodies the tradition created by these earlier women whose work we did not have space to represent. Because of space considerations also, we had in some cases to present excerpts from a few novels, as well as, in other cases, novellas and long short stories by major authors. We did this so that teachers can, if they wish, use NALW to trace the ways in which women writers of extended prose fictions have moved from the characteristically eighteenth-century modes of epistolary and (mock) sentimental fiction through the Gothic romance to realism, naturalism, and various forms of experimentation with narrative. Were we to attempt to construct a course or a section of a course dealing with this genre history, we would chose texts from among the following works:

Jane Austen, Love and Freindship
Elizabeth Cleghorn Gaskell, Cranford (excerpt)
Charlotte Brontë, Jane Eyre
George Eliot, "The Lifted Veil"
Harriet Wilson, Our Nig (excerpt)
Rebecca Harding Davis, Life in the Iron-Mills (novella)
Louise May Alcott, Work (excerpt)
Kate Chopin, The Awakening
Willa Cather, "Coming, Aphrodite!"
Gertrude Stein, "The Gentle Lena"
Tillie Olsen, "Tell Me a Riddle"
Doris Lessing, "To Room 19"

Edna O'Brien, "A Rose in the Heart"
Toni Morrison, The Bluest Eye


SHORT FICTION

Teachers who wish to use NALW as a text for
classes in women's prose fiction may also, of
course, decide to focus on the extraordinary
contributions of women to the development of the
short story in English.  Working trans-histor-
ically, such instructors might organize units
devoted to a number of subgenres or modes in
which female artists have written.  We would
suggest here that--although there is inevitably
some overlap--the short stories in NALW can be
divided into the following categories, categories
that to some extent reflect the historical evolution of the Romantic tale into the modern short
story:  fantasy (Gothic stories, supernatural
tales, science fiction, and allegories), regionalism (including ethnic fiction), realism, comedy, and experimentalism.


   Fantasy

   If teachers were to choose to devote a section of a course to an examination of women's
fantasy, they might want to start by proposing
long fictions like Jane Eyre and "The Lifted
Veil" as paradigms of the way in which women have
used what the critic Ellen Moers has called "female Gothic" to enact or explore distinctively
female rage at or dread of sexuality.  The Gothic, supernatural, and allegorical tales as well
as the science fiction included in NALW could be
used, however, both to support and to interrogate
Moers' hypothesis.  We would include the following works in this category:

   Mary Shelley, "The Mortal Immortal"
   Elizabeth Drew Stoddard, "Lemorne vs.
      Huell"
   Olive Schreiner, "A Little African Story"
   Charlotte Perkins Gilman, "The Yellow
      Wallpaper"
   May Sinclair, "The Bambino"
   Ellen Glasgow, "Jordan's End"

Isak Dinesen, "The Blank Page"
Radclyffe Hall, "Miss Ogilvy Finds
    Herself"
Mourning Dove, "The Origin of Diseases,"
    "Coyote Takes His Daughter as a Wife,"
    "Coyote Kills Owl-Woman"
Djuna Barnes, "Cassation"
Elizabeth Bowen, "The Demon Lover"
Shirley Jackson, "The Lottery"
Doris Lessing, "To Room 19"
Ursula K. Le Guin, "Sur"
Joanna Russ, "When It Changed"
Angela Carter, "The Company of Wolves"

Whether they are allegorical ("A Little African
Story," "The Blank Page"), Gothic ("The Mortal
Immortal," "The Bambino"), speculative ("The
Lottery," "Sur"), science fiction ("When It
Changed"), or simply fantasy ("Miss Ogilvy Finds
Herself"), almost all these stories appear in one
way or another to abrogate the conventions of
"realism" and thus to require from the reader
what Coleridge called "a willing suspension of
disbelief."  To be sure, a few are Gothic or
fantastic primarily in the sense that they parody
or incorporate certain Gothic devices or traditions, for instance the figure of the Satanic
hero ("Lemorne vs. Huell") and the atmosphere of
madness or of macabre dread ("The Yellow Wallpaper," "Cassation," "To Room 19"). Nevertheless,
taken together they suggest a background against
which even supposedly "realistic" fiction might
be read, for such tales as "Lemorne vs. Huell"
and "The Yellow Wallpaper" might be defined as
simultaneously fantastic and realistic.


Regionalism

    Just as feminist critics have speculated on
the centrality of the fantastic in the female
literary tradition, a number of scholars have
lately begun to explore the major contribution
women of letters have made to regional fiction.
Teachers who wish their students to examine the
ways in which women writers have invented and
employed representational strategies in order to
record what Virginia Woolf once called "the lives
of the obscure" might want to begin a course or a

section of a course with the discussion of a long
narrative like Kate Chopin's <u>The Awakening</u>. More
specifically, they might focus lectures and conversations on the possibility that regionalism
provided women writers with an opportunity to
portray those aspects of women's social history
that have been neglected by traditional historians or on the supplementary possibility that
regionalism--by transforming the writer into a
sort of anthropologist--allowed female artists to
undertake more general analyses of the very nature of culture. Moving on from Chopin's novel,
such teachers might consider some of the following works, all of which recreate the spirit of
such distinctive places as nineteenth-century New
England, small-town Canada, turn-of-the-century
Australia, southern Mississippi, or twentieth-
century Ghana:

Harriet Beecher Stowe, "The Minister's
    Housekeeper"
Sarah Orne Jewett, "The Town Poor"
Mary E. Wilkins Freeman, "Old Woman
    Magoun"
Olive Schreiner, "A Little African
    Story"
Ellen Glasgow, "Jordan's End"
Katherine Susannah Prichard, "The Cooboo"
Anzia Yezierska, "The Fat of the Land"
Katherine Anne Porter, "The Jilting of
    Granny Weatherall"
Zora Neale Hurston, "Sweat"
Eudora Welty, "The Wide Net"
Nadine Gordimer, "Town and Country
    Lovers"
Flannery O'Connor, "Good Country
    People"
Margaret Laurence, "The Loons"
Toni Cade Bambara, "My Man Bovanne"
Ama Ata Aidoo, "The Message"
Alice Walker, "Everyday Use"
Leslie Marmon Silko, "Lullabye"


Comedy

In the United States, at least, regionalism
has long been associated with humor.  The comic
works of Bret Harte and Mark Twain are, indeed,

specifically based on explorations and exploita-
tions of regional foibles as well as on the use
of such regionalist devices as dialect and tall
story.  But these men had female counterparts in
humorists like Fanny Fern and Frances Whicher,
women whose writings we would have included in
<u>NALW</u> had there been sufficient space.  Among the
regionalist selections we have included, however,
are texts which exploit many varieties of humor,
as both Welty's "The Wide Net" and Flannery
O'Connor's "Good Country People" reveal.  Yet
women working outside the regionalist tradition
have also obviously produced writings that could
be characterized as parody, satire, burlesque, or
comedy of manners.  Teachers who wish to develop
a unit on comic fiction might well begin with
Jane Austen's <u>Love</u> <u>and</u> <u>Freindship</u>, look also at
Elizabeth Gaskell's <u>Cranford</u>, and supplement
their short story assignments with readings of
women's comic verse (listed later in this manual).  Stories that might be studied would include:

> Edith Wharton, "The Angel at the Grave,"
>     "The Other Two"
> Katherine Mansfield, "The Daughters of
>     the Late Colonel"
> Rebecca West, "Indissoluble Matrimony"
> Dorothy Parker, "You Were Perfectly Fine"
> Eudora Welty, "The Wide Net"
> Muriel Spark, "The Fathers' Daughters"
> Grace Paley, "Enormous Changes at the
>     Last Minute"
> Flannery O'Connor, "Good Country People"
> Margaret Atwood, "Rape Fantasies"

## The Realistic

Both comedy and regionalism are, of course,
mimetic modes, closely associated with what is
ordinarily called fictional realism.  Regionalism
is, in fact, a subcategory of that mode, while
comedy--through such works as <u>Shamela</u>, <u>Joseph</u>
<u>Andrews</u>, and <u>Northanger</u> <u>Abbey</u>--contributed to the
rise of the realistic novel.  Thus, instructors
wishing to teach female realism might well choose
to draw works from the lists we have provided for
regionalism and comedy;  in addition, however,

beginning perhaps with analyses of some of the longer works and excerpts in <u>NALW</u> (notably <u>Our Nig</u>, <u>Life in the Iron-Mills</u>, "Coming, Aphrodite!," "To Room 19," "A Rose in the Heart," and "Tell Me a Riddle"), they could assign texts from the following list of stories:

> Elizabeth Drew Stoddard, "Lemorne <u>vs.</u> Huell"
> Charlotte Perkins Gilman, "The Yellow
>     Wallpaper"
> H.H. Richardson, "Two Hanged Women"
> Dorothy Richardson, "Death"
> Virginia Woolf, "The New Dress" and
>     "Slater's Pins Have No Points"
> Katherine Mansfield, "The Doll's House"
> Alice Munro, "Wild Swans"
> Jean Rhys, "On Not Shooting Sitting Birds"
> Meridel Le Sueur, "Annunciation"
> Carson McCullers, "Wunderkind"
> Kay Boyle, "Winter Night"

## Experimentalism

In attempting to represent reality "realistically," a number of writers have always, of course, resorted to forms of stylistic experimentation and innovation. Among male artists, the most obvious instances of such innovation would perhaps be Henry James's evolution of a sophisticated theory about point of view and James Joyce's development of so-called stream of consciousness. At the same time, men of letters--including Joyce himself--have often striven to subvert "realism" through the use of mythological allusion, surrealistic imagery, self-conscious allegorizing, and complex word play, all strategies which emphasize the literariness of every literary text. But women writers, too, have experimented not only with representational techniques designed to induce the illusion of real life but also with a number of other strategies that might be defined as in some sense antimimetic. In order to turn the attention of a class to the varieties of experimentation attempted by female authors, teachers might undertake a close study of such longer works as "Coming, Aphrodite!" (which embeds a nonrealistic legend in a supposedly realistic story), "The

Gentle Lena" (which employs incantatory, incre-
mental repetitions to create what Stein would
later call a "continuous present"), "Tell Me a
Riddle" (which represents a dying woman's stream
of consciousness through the use of allusions,
fragmented language, and associative leaps), and
The Bluest Eye (which parodies the naiveté of
children's literature while subverting that
naiveté through the construction of streams of
consciousness which contrast real life with dream
life).  They might then choose to assign works
from the following list;  these texts are, we
should note, more heterogeneous than some which
appear on our other lists--some present themselves as parables or allegories, others explore
stream of consciousness techniques or revisionary
storytelling methods--but their heterogeneity is,
we think, precisely a function of the diversity
of women's experimental ambition.

> Olive Schreiner, "A Little African Story"
> Charlotte Perkins Gilman, "The Yellow
>     Wallpaper"
> Dorothy Richardson, "Death"
> Gertrude Stein, "Ada"
> Virginia Woolf, "The New Dress" and
>     "Slater's Pins Have No Points"
> Isak Dinesen, "The Blank Page"
> Katherine Anne Porter, "The Jilting of
>     Granny Weatherall"
> Djuna Barnes, "Cassation"
> Angela Carter, "The Company of Wolves"

PERSONAL PROSE

Women have produced a good deal of expository and polemical prose.  More traditionally,
however, they have expressed themselves in such
supposedly "minor" or collateral forms as the
autobiography, the memoir, the journal, the
diary, and the letter.  Self-defining or confessional, these modes evolve from spiritual to
secular meditations, and, taken together,
throughout the six periods represented in NALW
they provide a startlingly vivid record of the
ways in which women, confined to privacy and
domesticity, have subversively submitted to what
would seem to be limitations in order to create

visions of expansiveness and transcendence. From
Julian of Norwich's cloistered dreams of God the
mother, Anne Bradstreet's imagery of heavenly
housekeeping, Rebecca Cox Jackson's almost surrealistic fantasies of culinary power, and Emily
Dickinson's cryptic communications with a master-
muse to Lillian Hellman's elegant examination of
grief and Maxine Hong Kingston's fantastic recon-
struction of a nameless ancestress, women's personal meditations and memoirs demonstrate a deep
culturally constructed female need to come to
terms with the origins and the history of the
self as well as a passionate and often impas-
sioned desire to dissolve the boundaries of that
self. At the same time, moreover, they provide
models for essays of self-definition that may
help students in writing classes as well as in
women's studies courses to understand the many
literary options available to them as they, too,
seek to articulate their identities. The following list may offer suggestions for the teacher of
composition or women's studies who wishes to
explore this self-analytic mode in some depth:

> Julian of Norwich, _A Book of Showings_
>   (excerpt)
> Margery Kempe, _The Book of Margery
>   Kempe_ (excerpt)
> Anne Bradstreet, "Meditations Divine
>   and Moral" (excerpt)
> Jane Lead, _A Fountain of Gardens_
>   (excerpt)
> Mary Rowlandson, _A Narrative of the
>   Captivity_ . . . (excerpt)
> Fanny Burney, _Diary_ (excerpt)
> Dorothy Wordsworth, _The Grasmere Jour-
>   nals_ (excerpt)
> Rebecca Cox Jackson, _Gifts of Power_
>   (excerpt)
> Linda Brent, _Incidents in the Life of a
>   Slave Girl_ (excerpt)
> Emily Dickinson, selected letters
> Alice James, _The Diary_
> Virginia Woolf, "22 Hyde Park Gate"
> Anaïs Nin, _Diary_ (excerpts)
> Lillian Hellman, _Pentimento_
>   (excerpt)
> Mary McCarthy, _Memoirs of a Catholic
>   Girlhood_ (excerpt)

Maya Angelou, I Know Why the Caged Bird
    Sings (excerpt)
Maxine Hong Kingston, No Name Woman


EXPOSITORY AND POLEMICAL PROSE

Although rational exposition and public
polemic are stereotypically associated with masculinity, women have a surprisingly strong tradition of composing such prose, and a tradition
which significantly antedates the rise of "offi-
cial" feminism.  Writing in many modes--speeches,
dialogues, letters, satires, visions, personal
testimonies, reviews, and critical essays--not-
able women and women of letters have long pro-
tested against the miseducation of girls, decon-
structed negative images of women, claimed a
parallel between racial and sexual oppression,
excavated their own history, and outlined dreams
of a transformed society.  In writing-oriented
courses, teachers might want to explore how
women's essays present arguments through strategies that might serve as models for student
themes.  In addition, composition teachers as
well as teachers of women's studies and women's
literature courses wishing to dramatize for students the richness and range of female-authored
expository and polemical prose might draw on the
following works:

Queen Elizabeth, "Speech to the Troops
    at Tilbury"
Margaret Cavendish, "Female Orations"
Mary Astell, A Serious Proposal to the
    Ladies (excerpt)
Lady Mary Wortley Montagu, "Letter to
    the Countess of Bute"
Mary Wollstonecraft, A Vindication of
    the Rights of Woman (excerpt)
Maria Edgeworth, Letters to Literary
    Ladies (excerpt)
Sojourner Truth, "Ain't I a Woman,"
    "What Time of Night It Is," "Keeping the
    Thing Going . . ."
Margaret Fuller, Woman in the Nineteenth
    Century (excerpt)
Elizabeth Cady Stanton, "Address to the
    New York Legislature"

Florence Nightingale, <u>Cassandra</u> (excerpt)
Olive Schreiner, <u>Woman</u> <u>and</u> <u>Labour</u> (excerpt)
Gertrude Stein, "Picasso"
Virginia Woolf, "<u>Jane</u> <u>Eyre</u> and <u>Wuthering</u>
    <u>Heights</u>," <u>A</u> <u>Room</u> <u>of</u> <u>One's</u> <u>Own</u> (excerpt
    on "Shakespeare's Sister"), "Professions for
    Women," and "A Woman's College from the
    Outside"
Zora Neale Hurston, "How It Feels to Be
    Colored Me"
Anaïs Nin, <u>Diary</u> (excerpt on Gender and
    Creativity)
Adrienne Rich, "When We Dead Awaken:
    Writing as Re-Vision"
Lorraine Hansberry, "In Defense of the
    Equality of Men"
Alice Walker, "In Search of Our Mothers'
    Gardens"

In addition, these readings could be supplemented
with assignments of a series of argumentative and
often consciously feminist poems which constitute
a strong ancillary tradition.  These could include any of the works in the following list:

Amelia Lanier, "Eve's Apology in Defense
    of Women"
Anne Bradstreet, "The Prologue," "In
    Honour of That High and Mighty Princess
    Queen Elizabeth of Happy Memory"
Mary Chudleigh, "To the Ladies"
Elizabeth Barrett Browning, <u>Aurora</u>
    <u>Leigh</u> (Book II)
Emily Dickinson, 401 ("What Soft--Cherubic
    Creatures--"), 732 ("She rose to His
    Requirement--dropt")
Alice Meynell, "A Father of Women"
Mary Elizabeth Coleridge, "The White Women"
Amy Lowell, "The Sisters"
Edna St. Vincent Millay, "Apostrophe to Man"
Louise Bogan, "Women"
Stevie Smith, "How Cruel Is the Story
    of Eve"
May Sarton, "My Sisters, O My Sisters"
Muriel Rukeyser, "Myth"
Judith Wright, "Eve to her Daughters"
Denise Levertov, "Hypocrite Women"
Carolyn Kizer, "Pro Femina"
Adrienne Rich, "Culture and Anarchy"

Marge Piercy, "The Token Woman"
Susan Griffin, "I Like to Think of
    Harriet Tubman"


DRAMA

What Yeats called "theater business, management of men" has plainly been problematic for
women authors, who, ordinarily  imprisoned in
privacy, had no access to precisely the spheres
of "business" and "management" that Yeats de-
plored.  No wonder, then, that Virginia Woolf's
parable of female literary frustration focused on
the suicidal history of Shakespeare's fictive
sister, Judith, who, Woolf wrote in A Room of
One's Own, was destroyed not only by societal
prohibitions of female dramatic ambition but also
by Nick Greene, an Elizabethan actor-manager and
master of "theater business."  Nevertheless,
despite Woolf's dark account, women of letters
from Aphra Behn and Susannah Centlivre to Augusta
Gregory, Susan Glaspell, Lillian Hellman, Lorraine Hansberry, Adrienne Kennedy, Megan Terry,
Caryl Churchill, and Marsha Norman have success-
fully composed and produced works for the stage.
To be sure, Mrs. Behn's bold assault on London's
theatrical scene earned her the reputation of
being a "shady lady."  Yet after her pioneering
efforts, a number of successors, especially in
the twentieth century, won significant reputa-
tions.  For reasons of space, we have not been
able to include such classics as The Little Foxes
and Raisin in the Sun. But for those teachers who
would like at least glancingly to consider women's contributions to drama, we have represented
important plays by Lady Augusta Gregory and Susan
Glaspell. Co-founder of the Abbey Theatre, Lady
Gregory knew at least as much as the Irish bard
did about "theater business, management of men,"
while Susan Glaspell, co-founder of the Province-
town Players (located on Cape Cod and in New York
City), helped shape two of the most influential
experimental theaters in America.  However, for
teachers who plan to allot extra time to the
issue of drama, we would suggest supplementing
our selections with such individual plays as
those represented in the following list:

Aphra Behn, The Lucky Chance
Susannah Centlivre, The Wonder
Gertrude Stein, Four Saints in Three Acts or
    The Mother of Us All
Edna St. Vincent Millay, Aria da Capo
Djuna Barnes, The Antiphon
Clare Booth Luce, The Women
Lillian Hellman, The Little Foxes, Toys in
    the Attic, or The Children's Hour
Lorraine Hansberry, A Raisin in the Sun or
    The Sign in Sidney Brustein's Window
Adrienne Kennedy, Funnyhouse of a Negro
Megan Terry, Approaching Simone or Calm
    Down, Mother
Ntozake Shange, For Colored Girls Who Have
    Considered Suicide/When the Rainbow Is Enuf
Caryl Churchill, Cloud Nine or Top Girls
Marsha Norman, Getting Out or 'Night, Mother

In addition, instructors may turn for other ideas
to a number of excellent anthologies, including
Fidelis Morgan's The Female Wits: Women Playwrights of the Restoration and Honor Moore's New
Women's Theater.

POETRY

    As we noted earlier, Virginia Woolf quite
cogently remarked in A Room of One's Own that
women's poetic impulses are still in some sense
"denied outlet." By this statement, we understand
Woolf to have meant not that women have failed to
compose excellent verse but rather that the female poetic tradition--rich and complex though it
is--is in a number of ways a problematic one
compared to the tradition of, say, female prose
fiction. Indeed, if we attempt to categorize
women's use of poetic genres in terms of the
conventional appearance of those genres in "mainstream" (male-authored) literary history, we find
extraordinary gaps and absences. Except for Elizabeth Barrett Browning's Aurora Leigh, for instance, there are few famous and successful pre-
twentieth-century epic poems composed by women.
One could not, so far as we can tell, retrieve a
woman's Beowulf, Faerie Queene, or Paradise Lost.
Moreover, so hegemonic a genre as the pastoral
elegy appears hardly to have been approached by
women poets. One could not, in our view, unearth

and reprint a female-authored "Lycidas," "Adonais," or "Thyrsis."

Even the history of women's use of the long poem, the sonnet or sonnet-sequence, and the dramatic or narrative poem seems somehow incongruent with male literary history. Women's long poems on meditative themes often do not "fit" the criteria established by the critic M. L. Rosenthal for, say, the modernist long poem or poemsequence; women's sonnets and sonnet-sequences seem to have been more frequently written after than during the Renaissance moment when so many great male-authored works in this mode were conceived; and women's narrative and dramatic poems often do not inscribe the ironies that are characteristic of, for instance, the Victorian dramatic monologue as practiced by Browning or Tennyson. Nevertheless, as we think our table of contents will reveal, women do have a strong and sure poetic history, some of which we can trace generically. Because of the difficulty of matching many female lyrics to traditional generic categories, however, our overview here must necessarily be truncated. Many of the poems in this book will in fact be listed under thematic rather than generic headings as a result of this problem. Here, though, for the teacher who might like to explore with a class precisely the generic paradoxes we have mentioned, we will try to propose ways in which some of the poems in NALW might be subsumed under certain relatively conventional generic categories, namely, the long poem, the sonnet or sonnet-sequence, the narrative or dramatic poem, the occasional poem, and the comic poem.

### The Long Poem

In considering women's use of the long poem, the first issue to address is obviously the question of how one defines a long poem. Traditionally, the long poem or (in Rosenthal's view) poem-sequence may be seen as differentiated from but somehow related to, on the one hand, such narrative forms as the epic (Paradise Lost, The Prelude), the allegorical romance (The Faerie Queene, "The Triumph of Life," "The Eve of St. Agnes," "Childe Roland to the Dark Tower Came"),

or the verse satire (<u>The</u> <u>Rape</u> <u>of</u> <u>the</u> <u>Lock</u>), and,
on the other hand, such essentially meditative
modes as the philosophical epistle (<u>An</u> <u>Essay</u> <u>on</u>
<u>Man</u>), the high Romantic ode ("Ode: Intimations of
Immortality," "Ode on a Grecian Urn"), and the
pastoral elegy ("Lycidas"). According to such
criteria, works like, for instance, <u>Song</u> <u>of</u>
<u>Myself</u> or <u>The</u> <u>Waste</u> <u>Land</u> would be said to com-
bine narrative and meditative modes with a vari-
ety of prosodic strategies in order to explore
many different aspects of a subject "in depth."

But while it is true that women's long poems
frequently attempt similar juxtapositions of
narration and meditation as well as (particularly
in the twentieth century) similarly complex techniques of versification, the relationship of
their extended texts to traditional forms is far
less clear. In fact, teachers who want to construct a unit on women's use of the long poem
might well begin by reviewing a group of traditional male-authored epics, odes, and elegies in
order to dramatize for their students the ways in
which women's works swerve from and revise generic conventions. Some analysis of women's historical relationship to poetic authority might then
be appropriate, since it is almost certainly the
case that women have had a problematic attitude
toward the long poem precisely because it would
have been considered "unfeminine" for a female
writer to adopt the traditionally male stance of
bard or prophet--the necessary stance, that is,
for the artist who undertakes the almost hieratic
task of composing an extended work in verse.

On the whole, as our selections for <u>NALW</u>
will suggest, female-authored long poems tend to
have an implicitly narrative core ("Eve's Apology," "The Disappointment," "The Runaway Slave at
Pilgrim's Point," "Brother and Sister") or else--
what is closely associated with such a core--an
"occasional" purpose; in other words, the woman
poet who is attempting an ambitiously elaborated
text appears to need to suggest that she is
either "just" telling a story or "just" writing a
kind of specialized "thank you" note to a patron,
patroness, or friend--both attitudes which may
well function to justify (or even disguise) the
author's stereotypically "unfeminine" literary
ambition.

We should perhaps note that the long poems

we have assembled for <u>NALW</u> are not only generically problematic in the ways we have already
mentioned but also because their overlap with
more distinctively conventional genres--in particular the sonnet-sequence and (obviously) the
narrative or dramatic verse--is quite striking.
(Thus some of the works named below will also
appear in other generic categories.)  Perhaps we
should add, too, that our speculations here are
highly provisional, since very little work has
been done on women's use of specific poetic genres. For this reason, though, teachers who undertake to investigate this subject with a class
will find that they and their students have an
unprecedented opportunity for creative thinking
in a new field. The following list of texts
included in <u>NALW</u> would thus be merely a place to
begin; if instructors wish to expand this unit in
order to explore the question of the female-
authored long poem more thoroughly, they could
obviously supplement our selections with assignments of complete works from which we have been
able only to present excerpts (e.g., <u>Aurora</u>
<u>Leigh</u>, <u>Trilogy</u>, <u>Circe/Mud</u> <u>Poems</u>).

> Mary Sidney Herbert, "To the Thrice Sacred
>     Queen Elizabeth"
> Amelia Lanier, "Eve's Apology" (excerpt)
> Anne Bradstreet, "In Honour of That High and
>     Mighty Princess Queen Elizabeth of Happy
>     Memory"
> Aphra Behn, "The Disappointment"
> Anne Finch, "The Spleen"
> Elizabeth Barrett Browning, "The Cry of the
>     Children," "The Runaway Slave at
>     Pilgrim's Point," <u>Aurora</u> <u>Leigh</u>
>     (excerpts), "A Curse for a Nation,"
>     "Mother and Poet"
> Emily Brontë, "The Prisoner" (excerpt)
> George Eliot, "Brother and Sister"
> Frances E. W. Harper, "Vashti"
> Christina Rossetti, "Goblin Market,"
>     "The Convent Threshold"
> Charlotte Mew, "The Quiet House," "The
>     Farmer's Bride"
> Amy Lowell, "The Sisters"
> Elinor Wylie, "Portrait in Black Paint"
> H.D., "Eurydice," <u>Tribute</u> <u>to</u> <u>the</u> <u>Angels</u>
>     (excerpt)

Marianne Moore, "The Jerboa," "Marriage"
Edna St. Vincent Millay, "Sonnets from
    an Ungrafted Tree"
Stevie Smith, "How Cruel Is the Story
    of Eve"
Elizabeth Bishop, "Roosters," "At the
    Fishhouses," "The Moose"
May Sarton, "My Sisters, O My Sisters"
Muriel Rukeyser, "Käthe Kollwitz"
Ruth Stone, "The Song of Absinthe
    Granny"
Eleanor Ross Taylor, "Welcome Eumenides"
Carolyn Kizer, "Pro Femina" (excerpt)
Anne Sexton, "O Ye Tongues" (excerpt)
Adrienne Rich, "Snapshots of a Daughter-
    in-law," "Diving into the Wreck,"
    "Culture and Anarchy"
Sylvia Plath, the Bee sequence ("The
    Bee Meeting," "The Arrival of the
    Bee Box," "Stings," "The Swarm," and
    "Wintering")
Diane Wakoski, "Blue Monday," "Ringless"
Louise Glück, "Dedication to Hunger"
Margaret Atwood, Circe/Mud Poems (excerpt)


The Sonnet or Sonnet-Sequence

    While the sonnet-sequence can and frequently
does function as a kind of narrative (Millay's
"Sonnets from an Ungrafted Tree," for instance,
tell the story of a problematic marriage while
Barrett Browning's Sonnets from the Portuguese
implicitly relate the progress of a love affair),
the sonnet itself is of course a specialized
verse form, one that since the Renaissance has
been associated with the Petrarchan conventions
of highly stylized self-examination first de-
ployed in England by Sidney, Drayton, and Shakespeare, and one that requires a mastery either of
the elegantly intricate Petrarchan rhyme-scheme
or of the looser but equally elegant Shakespear-
ean scheme. Interestingly, among poets represented in NALW, we find more women writing sonnets
and sonnet-sequences in the nineteenth and early
twentieth centuries than we do in the Renaissance
and seventeenth century, a fact that--like the
absence of traditional odes and pastoral elegies
in the female literary canon--suggests the dif-

fering relationships between tradition and the
male and female talents.

Nevertheless, those women who have written
sonnets have written them skillfully and, perhaps
more important, with a significant measure of
irony.  Historically, after all, it was the female beloved who received the "gift" of a sonnet-
sequence recounting her poet-lover's admiration
for her, his passionate hopes for their romance,
and his moments of suffering when he feared that
she might reject him.  From Elizabeth Barrett
Browning and Christina Rossetti to Elinor Wylie
and Edna St. Vincent Millay, however, women poets
have used the sonnet form to, in effect, turn the
tables on their lovers, articulating a specifically female point of view on the ritualized
courtship conventionally recorded in the male-
authored sonnet-sequence.  As Rossetti herself
noted in a prefatory note to her sequence "Monna
Innominata:  A Sonnet of Sonnets," "one can imagine many a lady as sharing her lover's poetic
aptitude . . . . Had such a lady spoken for
herself, the portrait left us might have appeared
more tender, if less dignified, than any drawn
even by a devoted friend."

Teachers wishing to explore the ways in
which women poets have historically used the
sonnet or sonnet-sequence for purposes comparable
to, yet (as Rossetti implies) different from,
those that inspired their male contemporaries
could choose assignments from the following sonnets and sonnet-sequences included in the anthology:

> Charlotte Smith, "Pressed by the Moon,
>     Mute Arbitress of Tides"
> Elizabeth Barrett Browning, "Grief,"
>     "To George Sand: A Desire," "To
>     George Sand:  A Recognition," "Hiram
>     Powers' 'Greek Slave,'" Sonnets from
>     the Portuguese (excerpts)
> George Eliot, "Brother and Sister"
> Christina Rossetti, "After Death," "A
>     Soul," "The World," "Dead Before Death,"
>     "Cobwebs," "A Triad," "In an Artist's
>     Studio"
> Anna Hempstead Branch, Sonnets from a
>     Lock Box (excerpts)
> Elinor Wylie, "One Person" (excerpt)

Edna St. Vincent Millay, "Oh, Oh, you
    will be sorry for that word!", "I,
    being born a woman and distressed,"
    "Sonnets from an Ungrafted Tree," "Women
    have loved before as I love now," "Oh,
    sleep forever in the Latmian cave," "I
    too beneath your moon, almighty Sex"
Muriel Rukeyser, "Who in One Lifetime,"
    "To Be a Jew in the Twentieth Century"
    (from "Letter to the Front")
Margaret Walker, "Whores"
Adrienne Rich, from Twenty-one Love
    Poems (revisionary, quasi-sonnets)

In addition, teachers might wish to supplement
the selections available in NALW with more exten-
ded readings in such cycles as Lady Mary Wroth's
Pamphilia to Amphilanthus, Christina Rossetti's
"Monna Innominata," Elizabeth Barrett Browning's
Sonnets from the Portuguese, Anna Hempstead
Branch's Sonnets from a Lock Box, and Elinor
Wylie's "One Person."


The Narrative or Dramatic Poem

    Although there is considerable overlap be-
tween the texts we have included in the category
"The Long Poem" and those that fall into the
larger category of "The Narrative or Dramatic
Poem," we think it may be useful if we list here
all the works in NALW that could be defined as
narrative or dramatic verses, since a number of
the lyrics in the volume do have narrative or
dramatic structures which might be worth examining with a class.  Some, for instance, are ballads or ballad-like (such as, e.g., Margaret
Walker's "Kissie Lee" or Ruth Stone's "The Song
of Absinthe Granny"); others are traditional
dramatic monologues or soliloquies (for instance,
Barrett Browning's "The Runaway Slave at Pilgrim's Point," Charlotte Mew's "The Farmer's
Bride," or Eleanor Ross Taylor's "Welcome Eumenides"); others are "confessional" poems--reminis-
cences and self-defining or self-mythologizing
narratives (for instance, Plath's "Daddy" or
Sexton's "O Ye Tongues"), while still others,
less generically clear-cut, nevertheless tell or
allude to stories whose similarities and differ-

ences might be interesting to examine in a course
devoted to, say, the interpretation of poetry.
These narrative and dramatic poems include:

Aphra Behn, "The Willing Mistress,"
   "The Disappointment"
Anne Finch, "The Circuit of Apollo"
Mary Wortley Montagu, "Epistle from
   Mrs. Yonge to Her Husband"
Elizabeth Barrett Browning, "The
   Runaway Slave at Pilgrim's Point,"
   Aurora Leigh (excerpts), "Mother
   and Poet"
Emily Brontë, "F. de Samara to A.G.A.,"
   "R. Alcona to J. Brenzaida," "The
   Prisoner"
George Eliot, "Brother and Sister"
Frances E. W. Harper, "Aunt Chloe's
   Politics," "Learning to Read," "Vashti"
Emily Dickinson, 465 ("I heard a Fly
   buzz--when I died--"), 579 ("I had
   been hungry, all the Years--"), 593
   ("I think I was enchanted"), 732 ("She
   rose to His Requirement--dropt"), 754 ("My
   Life had stood--a Loaded Gun--"), 1670 ("In
   Winter in my Room")
Christina Rossetti, "Shut-Out," "The
   Convent Threshold," "Goblin Market"
Mary Elizabeth Coleridge, "The Other
   Side of a Mirror," "The Devil's
   Funeral," "The Witch"
Charlotte Mew, "The Quiet House," "The
   Farmer's Bride"
H.D., "Eurydice," Tribute to the Angels
   (excerpt)
Edith Sitwell, "En Famille," "Sir
   Beelzebub," "Serenade:  Any Man to
   Any Woman"
Edna St. Vincent Millay, "Sonnets from
   an Ungrafted Tree," "The Buck in the
   Snow," "Rendezvous," "The Fitting"
Louise Bogan, "The Crossed Apple,"
   "Medusa," "Cassandra," "The Sleeping
   Fury," "Evening in the Sanitarium,"
   "The Dream"
Ruth Pitter, "Old Nelly's Birthday,"
   "Yorkshire Wife's Saga"
Stevie Smith, "Papa Love Baby," "Not
   Waving but Drowning," "How Cruel Is

the Story of Eve"
Kathleen Raine, "Isis Wanderer," "Kore
   in Hades"
Elizabeth Bishop, "In the Waiting
   Room," "The Moose"
Josephine Miles, "Doll," "Parent,"
   "Bureau 2," "Concert"
May Sarton, "Letter from Chicago"
Muriel Rukeyser, "Boy with His Hair Cut
   Short," "The Birth of Venus," "The
   Poem as Mask," "Käthe Kollwitz,"
   "Myth"
Ruth Stone, "In an Iridescent Time,"
   "Periphery," "The Song of Absinthe
   Granny"
Margaret Walker, "Molly Means," "Kissie
   Lee"
Judith Wright, "The Sisters," "Request
   to a Year," "Naked Girl and Mirror"
Gwendolyn Brooks, "The Bean Eaters,"
   "We Real Cool," "Jessie Mitchell's
   Mother," "The Crazy Woman," "Bronzeville
   Woman in a Red Hat," "Riot"
May Swenson, "Bleeding"
Eleanor Ross Taylor, "Welcome Eumenides"
Denise Levertov, "The Goddess"
Carolyn Kizer, "Semele Recycled"
Anne Sexton, "Her Kind," "The Moss of
   His Skin," "Housewife," "O Ye Tongues"
   (excerpt)
Adrienne Rich, "Diving into the Wreck,"
   "Phantasia for Elvira Shateyev,"
   "Culture and Anarchy"
Sylvia Plath, "The Disquieting Muses,"
   "Parliament Hill Fields," the Bee
   sequence, "Daddy," "Lady Lazarus"
Lucille Clifton, mary poems
Marge Piercy, "The Friend"
Diane Wakoski, "Belly Dancer," "Blue
   Monday"
Margaret Atwood, <u>Circe/Mud</u> <u>Poems</u>
   (excerpts)
Judy Grahn, "The Common Woman"
   (excerpts)
Louise Glück, "Dedication to Hunger,"
   "Horse"

Instructors deciding to devote some time to
the issues raised by these works might want to

compare women's verse narratives to such male-
authored narrative texts as Coleridge's "The Rime
of the Ancient Mariner," Keats's "La Belle Dame
Sans Merci" or his "The Eve of St. Agnes," Tennyson's "Ulysses" or "Tithonus," Browning's "My
Last Duchess" or "Fra Lippo Lippi," T. S. Eliot's
"The Love Song of J. Alfred Prufrock," and Robert
Lowell's "Memories of West Street and Lepke" or
"Skunk Hour."  In addition, they might wish to
supplement readings of these works with more
extensive assignments from the ballads and narratives of Barrett Browning and Rossetti or from
such texts as Gwendolyn Brooks' In the Mecca,
Sexton's The Death Notebooks, or Plath's
Ariel.


The Occasional Poem

     As we noted earlier, from the Renaissance to
the present a surprising number of women have
written "occasional" poems--verses meant to respond to a specific person or event.  Honoring
patrons and patronesses, celebrating significant
moments of transformation or happiness, excoria-
ting political foes, female poets frequently
appear to have been released into literary ambition (and verse) by the exigencies of particular
circumstances, circumstances whose pressure could
be said to have "required" utterances that might
otherwise have seemed unsuitable, even indecor-
ous, for women.  Perhaps precisely because the
"occasional" poem so often did appear to be a
response to a situation that demanded commentary,
women writers could use the form not only to
speak but also to speak out on subjects that
would ordinarily be forbidden:  public policy
(e.g., slavery, war), female oppression, and
other controversial topics.
     In using the occasional poem for such rea-
sons, these artists were not, of course, doing
anything very different from what their male
contemporaries would have done; yet they were,
for women, taking comparatively radical action.
Thus teachers wishing to explore this form as it
is represented on the list below might well
choose to contextualize women's occasional verses
from NALW with prose works in the anthology--
letters, essays, journal entries, speeches, and

other polemics--that were also written in response to specific, often highly politicized
situations.  Occasional poems in NALW include:

Mary Sidney Herbert, "To the Thrice
    Sacred Queen Elizabeth"
Anne Bradstreet, "The Prologue," "In
    Honour of that High and Mighty
    Princess Queen Elizabeth of Happy Memory,"
    "A Letter to Her Husband," "Here
    Follows Some Verses Upon the Burning
    of Our House"
Katherine Philips, "To My Excellent
    Lucasia"
Aphra Behn, "To the Fair Clarinda"
Anne Killigrew, "Upon the Saying that
    My Verses Were Made by Another"
Anne Finch, "The Introduction," "A
    Letter to Daphnis," "Friendship
    between Ephelia and Ardelia," "The
    Answer"
Mary Wortley Montagu, "Epistle from
    Mrs. Yonge to Her Husband"
Phillis Wheatley, "On Being Brought
    from Africa to America," "To the
    Right Honourable William, Earl of
    Dartmouth"
Elizabeth Barrett Browning, "To George
    Sand:  A Desire," "To George Sand:
    A Recognition," "The Cry of the
    Children," "A Curse for a Nation,"
    "Mother and Poet"
Frances E. W. Harper, "Learning to
    Read"
Emily Dickinson, 312 ("Her--'last
    poems'--"), 593 ("I think I was
    enchanted"), 1562 ("Her Losses make
    our Gains ashamed--")
Christina Rossetti, "Enrica, 1865"
Alice Meynell, "A Father of Women,"
    "The Sunderland Children"
Edith Sitwell, "Lullaby," "Serenade:
    Any Man to Any Woman"
Edna St. Vincent Millay, "To Inez
    Milholland," "Apostrophe to Man"
Elizabeth Bishop, "The Man-Moth,"
    "Invitation to Miss Marianne Moore,"
    "Pink Dog"
Josephine Miles, "Why We Are Late"

May Sarton, "Letter from Chicago"
Muriel Rukeyser, "Who in One Lifetime,"
    "Letter to the Front" (excerpt),
    "The Power of Suicide"
Gwendolyn Brooks, "Riot"
Denise Levertov, "A Note to Olga
    (1966)," "Divorcing"
Maxine W. Kumin, "How It Is," "Making
    the Jam Without You"
Anne Sexton, "Somewhere in Africa,"
    "Sylvia's Death"
Adrienne Rich, "From a Survivor,"
    "Phantasia for Elvira Shatayev"
Sylvia Plath, the Bee sequence
Anne Stevenson, "Re-reading Jane"
Kamala Das, "An Introduction"
Erica Jong, "Alcestis on the Poetry
    Circuit"
Susan Griffin, "I Like to Think of
    Harriet Tubman"

In addition, teachers could assign supplementary
works, selected from women's occasional (and
often political) verses; possible readings could
include excerpts from Barrett Browning's Casa
Guidi Windows or Letters Before Congress, from
Muriel Rukeyser's "Letter to the Front," from
Gwendolyn Brooks's Riot, and from Adrienne Rich's
The Will to Change or Leaflets.


Comic Verse

    Women are often, stereotypically, said to
have "no sense of humor," but in fact--as not
only much prose but much verse in NALW will
reveal--the female literary tradition includes an
exhilarating vein of witty writing.  Particularly
during the Restoration and in the twentieth
century, women poets have allowed themselves,
both gently and savagely, to poke fun at prevail-
ing cultural and psychological phenomena, including social hypocrisy, male pomposity, and (even)
female "vanity."  Indeed, although few women
artists produced verse satires characterized by
the saeva indignatio of Swift or the sardonic
bathos of Pope, a number composed verses whose
elegantly formulated comedy deflated pretensions
as surely as did the works written by their male

contemporaries.    In particular, from the high-
spirited wit of Aphra Behn to the cynical humor
of Dorothy Parker, from the loving burlesques of
Frances E. W. Harper to the mordant morbidity of
Stevie Smith and the ferocious grotesquerie of
Sylvia Plath or Erica Jong, women poets have
satirized themselves, along with their male and
female associates, with verve and imagination.
     Teachers wishing to explore with a class the
modes in which women humorists have worked could
easily put together a unit on female comedy which
would combine studies in short fiction (see our
listings of comic short stories, earlier) with
examinations of women's comic verse (and, indeed,
drama).  The anthology offers a variety of verse
selections, including the following:

> Aphra Behn, "The Willing Mistress,"
>     "The Disappointment," "On Her Loving
>     Two Equally"
> Anne Finch, "The Circuit of Apollo,"
>     "The Answer"
> Charlotte Smith, "Thirty-eight"
> Frances E. W. Harper, "Aunt Chloe's
>     Politics," "Learning to Read"
> Anna Wickham, "Dedication of the Cook"
> Elinor Wylie, "Portrait in Black Paint"
> Edith Sitwell, "En Famille," "Sir
>     Beelzebub"
> Marianne Moore, "Silence," "O To Be a
>     Dragon"
> Edna St. Vincent Millay, "First Fig,"
>     "Second Fig," "Rendezvous"
> Louise Bogan, "Several Voices Out of a
>     Cloud"
> Dorothy Parker, "Résumé," "One Perfect
>     Rose," "News Item," "Song of One of
>     the Girls," "A Pig's-Eye View of
>     Literature"   (excerpts)
> Ruth Pitter, "The Irish Patriarch"
> Stevie Smith, "This Englishwoman,"
>     "Lord Barrenstock," "Souvenir de
>     Monsieur Poop"
> Josephine Miles, "Dear Frank, Here is a
>     Poem," "Bureau 2," "Concert"
> Muriel Rukeyser, "Myth"
> Ruth Stone, "The Song of Absinthe
>     Granny"
> Gwendolyn Brooks, "We Real Cool"

May Swenson, "Bleeding"
Carolyn Kizer, "Pro Femina" (excerpt)
Sylvia Plath, "Daddy," "Lady Lazarus"
Fleur Adcock, "Against Coupling"
Lucille Clifton, "Admonitions"
Marge Piercy, "The Token Woman"
Diane Wakoski, "Ringless"
Margaret Atwood, "[You Fit into Me]"
Erica Jong, "Castration of the Pen,"
    "Alcestis on the Poetry Circuit"

Readings in <u>NALW</u> might be supplemented with
further assignments in the verse of Aphra Behn,
Dorothy Parker, Stevie Smith, Erica Jong, and
others, together with studies of such nineteenth-
century poems as Barrett Browning's "A Man's
Requirements" and Christina Rossetti's "No Thank
You, John," as well as the works of humorists
like Fanny Fern and Frances Whicher.

## THEMES OF GENDER

Because of the richness and complexity of its table of contents, NALW is ideally suited for courses organized along thematic lines. We have therefore assembled on the following pages a series of thematic tables designed to define clusters of recurrent images and ideas. Any one such cluster could be employed to organize at least a unit of a course, and it is possible as well that a complete course could be based on a series of related clusters--for instance, the tables subsumed under the heading "The Female Life Cycle" or the tables entitled "General Politics" and "Feminist Politics."

Of course the thematic categories we have formulated are neither exclusive nor exhaustive. In a number of cases, a poem or story will appear on several lists and, in addition, other lists could probably be made, reflecting the interests of individual instructors and students. The categories we have chosen are meant, however, to provide a series of starting points for those dealing with unfamiliar material. They include:

> The Female Life Cycle (Growing Up Female,
>     The Family, The Single Woman, Marriage,
>     Motherhood, Aging, and Death)
> Women and Sexuality (Heterosexual Eroticism,
>     Lesbianism)
> Women and Nature
> Women and Politics (General Politics,
>     Feminist Politics)
> Gender and Race
> Women and Work (Domesticity, Economics)
> Women and Spirituality
> Women and Madness
> Women and Violence
> Female Communities
> Women on Specific Women
> Myths of Femaleness
> Women and Creativity

We suspect that teachers working with these categories may want to begin by tracing the evo-

lution of an image or idea from earlier periods
to the present, in order to explore, on the one
hand, the ways in which a theme may have remained
consistent over time, or, on the other hand, the
ways in which a theme has been transformed by
differing cultural circumstances.  The image of
Eve, for instance, has always been of interest to
women writers, as have imaginings of female community, but the concepts of, for example, both
lesbianism and work in the public sphere have
been radically revised in recent years.  While
examining such historical continuities and discontinuities, moreover, teachers might wish to
supplement readings in <u>NALW</u> with assignments of
relevant theoretical or sociocultural material.
Studies of "Growing Up Female" might be enriched
by references to Freud's "Female Sexuality"
(1931), Chodorow's <u>The Reproduction of Mothering</u>,
and the writings of other psychoanalysts, sociol-
ogists, and anthropologists (e.g., Karen Horney,
Melanie Klein, and Margaret Mead).  Units on
"Feminist Politics" might be supported by readings in the history of the women's movement
(e.g., texts by Strachey, Flexner, and Rowbotham).  Analyses of "Women and Spirituality" might
be strengthened by assignments from such books as
Mary Daly's <u>Beyond God the Father</u>, Rosemary
Ruether's <u>Women of Spirit</u>, Naomi Goldenberg's <u>The
Changing of the Gods</u>, and Carol Christ's <u>Diving
Deep and Surfacing</u>.
    We should add, however, that whether or not
teachers choose to supplement assignments in <u>NALW</u>
with such outside readings they will almost
certainly be able to break down some of our
categories into subcategories which students
might profitably explore both individually and in
groups.  The thematic heading "General Politics," for example, subsumes a group of texts
dealing specifically with women and war, while
the heading "Feminist Politics" subsumes a set
of texts on women and education.  Given that such
a range of topics and ideas has been addressed
throughout women's literary history, we are con-
fident that teachers and their classes will
identify many more, and we hope that you will
send us suggestions as they occur to you.

THE FEMALE LIFE CYCLE

Growing Up Female

Jane Austen, <u>Love and Freindship</u>
Elizabeth Barrett Browning, "The Cry of the
    Children," from <u>Aurora Leigh</u>, Books I
    and II
Charlotte Brontë, <u>Jane Eyre</u>
Emily Brontë, "Tell me, tell me, smiling
    child"
George Eliot, "Brother and Sister"
Harriet Wilson, from <u>Our Nig</u>
Emily Dickinson, 959 ("A loss of something
    ever felt I--")
Christina Rossetti, "Shut Out," "Goblin
    Market"
Mary E. Wilkins Freeman, "Old Woman Magoun"
Olive Schreiner, "A Little African Story"
Virginia Woolf, "22 Hyde Park Gate"
Katherine Mansfield, "The Doll's House"
Edna St. Vincent Millay, "Childhood Is the
    Kingdom . . ."
Stevie Smith, "The Wanderer"
Kay Boyle, "Winter Night"
Elizabeth Bishop, "In the Waiting Room"
Josephine Miles, "Doll," "Parent"
Mary McCarthy, from <u>Memories of a Catholic
    Girlhood</u>
Carson McCullers, "Wunderkind"
Flannery O'Connor, "Good Country People"
Edna O'Brien, "A Rose in the Heart"
Toni Morrison, <u>The Bluest Eye</u>
Joyce Carol Oates, "Where Are You
    Going? . . ."
Louise Glück, "Dedication to Hunger"


The Family:  Father-Daughter Relationships

Anne Bradstreet, "To Her Father with Some
    Verses"
Alice Meynell, "Parentage," "A Father of
    Women," "The Sunderland Children"
Mary E. Wilkins Freeman, "Old Woman Magoun"
Edith Wharton, "The Angel at the Grave"
Katherine Mansfield, "The Daughters of the
    Late Colonel"
Mourning Dove, "Coyote Takes His Daughter as

a Wife"
Stevie Smith, "Papa Loves Baby"
Josephine Miles, "Parent"
Muriel Spark, "The Fathers' Daughters"
Grace Paley, "Enormous Changes at the Last
    Minute"
Anne Sexton, "The Moss of His Skin"
Margaret Laurence, "The Loons"
Toni Morrison, The Bluest Eye
Sylvia Plath, "The Colossus," "Daddy"


The Family:  Siblings

Dorothy Wordsworth, from The Grasmere Jour-
    nals
George Eliot, "Brother and Sister"
Alice James, from The Diary
Sarah Orne Jewett, "The Town Poor"
Anzia Yezierska, "The Fat of the Land"
Edith Sitwell, "En Famille"
Katherine Mansfield, "The Daughters of the
    Late Colonel," "The Doll's House"
Mourning Dove, "The Origin of Diseases"
Judith Wright, "The Sisters"
Denise Levertov, "A Note to Olga"
Toni Morrison, The Bluest Eye


The Family:  Mothers (Having a Mother or
Matrilineage)

Julian of Norwich, from A Book of Showings
Elizabeth Barrett Browning, excerpt from
    Book I of Aurora Leigh
Edna St. Vincent Millay, "The Courage that
    My Mother Had"
Kay Boyle, "Winter Night"
Kathleen Raine, "Heirloom"
Dorothy Livesay, "Green Rain"
Ruth Stone, "In an Iridescent Time"
Margaret Walker, "Lineage"
Maya Angelou, from I Know Why the Caged Bird
    Sings
Edna O'Brien, "A Rose in the Heart"
Adrienne Rich, "Snapshots of a Daughter-in-
    Law"
Toni Morrison, The Bluest Eye
Sylvia Plath, "The Disquieting Muses,"

"Medusa,"
Audre Lorde, "From the House of Yemanjá"
Maxine Hong Kingston, "No Name Woman"
Alice Walker, "In Search of Our Mothers'
    Gardens," "Everyday Use"


## The Single Woman

Elizabeth Gaskell, from <u>Cranford</u>
Sarah Orne Jewett, "The Town Poor"
Virginia Woolf, "The New Dress," "Slater's
    Pins Have No Points"
Katherine Mansfield, "The Daughters of the
    Late Colonel"
Fleur Adcock, "Against Coupling"


## Marriage

Anne Bradstreet, "A Letter to Her Husband"
Anne Finch, "A Letter to Daphnis"
Lady Mary Wortley Montagu, "Epistle from
    Mrs. Yonge to Her Husband"
Mary Shelley, "The Mortal Immortal"
Elizabeth Barrett Browning, excerpt from
    <u>Aurora Leigh</u>, Book I
Harriet Beecher Stowe, "The Minister's
    Housekeeper"
George Eliot, "The Lifted Veil"
Emily Dickinson, 732 ("She rose to His
    Requirement--dropt"), 1072 ("Title
    divine--is mine!"), 1737 ("Rearrange a
    'Wife's' affection!")
Mary Elizabeth Coleridge, "Marriage"
Edith Wharton, "The Other Two"
Ellen Glasgow, "Jordan's End"
Gertrude Stein, "The Gentle Lena"
Susan Glaspell, "Trifles"
Anna Wickham, "Divorce"
Marianne Moore, "Marriage"
Edna St. Vincent Millay, "Sonnets from an
    Ungrafted Tree"
Rebecca West, "Indissoluble Matrimony"
Dorothy Parker, "You Were Perfectly Fine"
Zora Neale Hurston, "Sweat"
Eudora Welty, "The Wide Net"
Stevie Smith, "Lightly Bound"
Doris Lessing, "To Room 19"

Denise Levertov, "The Ache of Marriage,"
    "Abel's Bride," "Divorcing"
Adrienne Rich, "Snapshots of a Daughter-in-
    Law," "From a Survivor," "Phantasia for
    Elvira Shatayev"
Toni Morrison, The Bluest Eye
Sylvia Plath, "Daddy," "Stings"
Anne Stevenson, "Marriage," "Respectable
    House"
Louise Glück, "Horse"


Motherhood (Being a Mother)

Anne Bradstreet, from Meditations, Divine
    and Moral
Mary Rowlandson, from A Narrative of the
    Captivity . . .
Elizabeth Barrett Browning, "Mother and
    Poet"
Alice Meynell, "Parentage"
Kate Chopin, The Awakening
Mary E. Wilkins Freeman, "Old Woman Magoun"
Charlotte Perkins Gilman, "The Yellow
    Wallpaper"
May Sinclair, "The Bambino"
Gertrude Stein, "The Gentle Lena"
Katharine Susannah Prichard, "The Cooboo"
Anzia Yezierska, "The Fat of the Land"
Marianne Moore, "The Paper Nautilus"
Djuna Barnes, "Cassation"
Ruth Pitter, "Yorkshire Wife's Saga"
Meridel Le Sueur, "Annunciation"
Kay Boyle, "Winter Night"
Dorothy Livesay, "The Children's Letters"
Elizabeth Bishop, "Pink Dog"
Eudora Welty, "The Wide Net"
Tillie Olsen, "Tell Me a Riddle"
Ruth Stone, "The Song of Absinthe Granny"
Gwendolyn Brooks, "The Mother," "Jessie
    Mitchell's Mother"
Denise Levertov, "The Son"
Maxine Kumin, "The Envelope," "Making the
    Jam Without You"
Anne Sexton, "In Celebration of My Uterus"
Edna O'Brien, "A Rose in the Heart"
Toni Morrison, The Bluest Eye
Sylvia Plath, "Nick and the Candlestick,"
    "Parliament Hill Fields," the Bee

sequence, "Edge"
Audre Lorde, "Now That I Am Forever with
   Child"
Margaret Atwood, "Spelling"
Toni Cade Bambara, "My Man Bovanne"
Maxine Hong Kingston, "No Name Woman"
Ama Ata Aidoo, "The Message"
Louise Glück, "Illuminations"
Alice Walker, "Everyday Use"
Leslie Marmon Silko, "Lullabye"


## Aging

Charlotte Smith, "Thirty-eight"
Mary Shelley, "The Mortal Immortal"
Sarah Orne Jewett, "The Town Poor"
Anzia Yezierska, "The Fat of the Land"
Katherine Anne Porter, "The Jilting of
   Granny Weatherall"
Ruth Pitter, "Old Nelly's Birthday"
Josephine Miles, "Concert"
Tillie Olsen, "Tell Me a Riddle"
Ruth Stone, "Periphery," "The Song of
   Absinthe Granny"
Judith Wright, "The Sisters"
Grace Paley, "Enormous Changes at the Last
   Minute"
Leslie Marmon Silko, "Lullabye"


## Death

Emily Brontë, "R. Alcona to J. Brenzaida,"
   "No coward soul is mine"
Emily Dickinson, 258 ("There's a certain
   Slant of light"), 280 ("I felt a Funeral,
   in my Brain"), 341 ("After great pain, a
   formal feeling comes--"), 465 ("I heard a
   Fly buzz--when I died--"), 510 ("It was
   not Death, for I stood up"), 712 ("Because
   I could not stop for Death--"), 1445
   ("Death is the supple Suitor")
Christina Rossetti, "Song" ("When I am dead,
   my dearest"), "After Death," "Dead Before
   Death," "Up-Hill"
Alice James, from the <u>Diary</u>
Kate Chopin, <u>The Awakening</u>
Dorothy Richardson, "Death"

H.D., "Euridice"
Edith Sitwell, "Where is all the bright
    company gone--"
Katherine Anne Porter, "The Jilting of
    Granny Weatherall"
Edna St. Vincent Millay, "Sonnets from an
    Ungrafted Tree"
Dorothy Parker, "Résumé"
Elizabeth Bowen, "The Demon Lover"
Stevie Smith, "Not Waving but Drowning"
Kay Boyle, "Winter Night"
Lillian Hellman, "Pentimento"
May Sarton, "Letter from Chicago"
Muriel Rukeyser, "The Power of Suicide"
Tillie Olsen, "Tell Me a Riddle"
Judith Wright, "Half-Caste Girl"
Doris Lessing, "To Room 19"
Maxine Kumin, "The Envelope"
Anne Sexton, "The Moss of His Skin,"
    "Somewhere in Africa," "Sylvia's Death"
Adrienne Rich, "From a Survivor"
Sylvia Plath, "Daddy," "Lady Lazarus,"
    "Edge"
Diane Wakoski, "Blue Monday"
Joyce Carol Oates, "Where Are You
    Going? . . ."


WOMEN AND SEXUALITY

Heterosexual Eroticism

Margery Kempe, from The Book of Margery
    Kempe
Queen Elizabeth I, "On Monsieur's Departure"
Aphra Behn, "The Willing Mistress," "Love
    Armed," "The Disappointment," "On her
    Loving Two Equally"
Jane Austen, Love and Freindship
Elizabeth Barrett Browning, from Sonnets
    from the Portuguese
Charlotte Brontë, Jane Eyre
Emily Brontë, "F. de Samara to A.G.A"
    ("Light up thy halls!")
Emily Dickinson, 211 ("Come slowly--Eden!"),
    249 ("Wild Nights--Wild Nights!"), 322
    ("There came a Day at Summer's full"),
    754 ("My Life had stood--a Loaded
    Gun--"), 670 ("In Winter in my Room"),

letters 233, 248

Christina Rossetti, "Song" ("When I am dead, my dearest"), "A Birthday," "The Convent Threshold," "Goblin Market," "In an Artist's Studio"

Kate Chopin, The Awakening

Charlotte Mew, "The Farmer's Bride"

Elinor Wylie, "One Person"

H.D., "Fragment 36"

Edna St. Vincent Millay, "Oh, Oh, you will be sorry for that word!," "I, being born a woman and distressed," "Women have loved before as I love now," "Oh, sleep forever in the Latmian cave," "Rendez-vous," "The Fitting," "I too beneath your moon, almighty Sex"

Jean Rhys, "On Not Shooting Sitting Birds"

Elizabeth Bowen, "The Demon Lover"

Margaret Walker, "Kissie Lee," "Whores"

Judith Wright, "Naked Girl and Mirror," "Rosina Alcona to Julius Brenzaida"

Grace Paley, "Enormous Changes at the Last Minute"

Denise Levertov, "Eros at Temple Stream"

Carolyn Kizer, "Semele Recycled"

Toni Morrison, The Bluest Eye

Alice Munro, "Wild Swans"

Fleur Adcock, "Against Coupling"

Joanna Russ, "When It Changed"

Diane Wakoski, "Blue Monday," "Belly Dancer"

Joyce Carol Oates, "Where Are You Going? . . ."

Margaret Atwood,  "Rape Fantasies," "[You Fit into Me]"

Louise Glück, "Horse"

Angela Carter, "The Company of Wolves"


Lesbianism

Aphra Behn, "To the Fair Clarinda, who Made Love to Me . . ."

H.H. Richardson, "Two Hanged Women"

Amy Lowell, "The Letter," "Venus Transiens," "Madonna of the Evening Flowers," "The Weather-cock Points South," "Opal," "A Decade"

Gertrude Stein, "Ada"

Virginia Woolf, "Slater's Pins Have No

Points"
Radclyffe Hall, "Miss Ogilvy Finds Herself"
Anaïs Nin, Diary entry on June Miller
Elizabeth Bishop, "One Art"
Adrienne Rich, from Twenty-One Love Poems,
    "Culture and Anarchy"
Audre Lorde, "On a Night of the Full Moon"
Joanna Russ, "When It Changed"
Judy Grahn, "in the place . . ."


WOMEN AND NATURE

Anne Finch, "To the Nightingale," "A
    Noctural Reverie"
Charlotte Smith, "Pressed by the Moon, Mute
    Arbitress of Tides"
Dorothy Wordsworth, from The Grasmere Jour-
    nals, "Peaceful Our Valley, Fair and
    Green"
Emily Brontë, "A Day Dream," "Often rebuked,
    yet always back returning"
Emily Dickinson, 258 ("There's a certain
    Slant of light"), 322 ("There came a Day
    at Summer's full"), 392 ("Through the
    Dark Sod--as Education--"), 465 ("I heard
    a Fly buzz--when I died--"), 722 ("Sweet
    Mountains--Ye tell Me no lie--"), 986 ("A
    narrow Fellow in the Grass"), 1138 ("A
    Spider sewed at Night"), 1657 ("Eden is
    that old-fashioned House"), 1670 ("In
    Winter in my Room"), 1705 ("Volcanoes be
    in Sicily")
Elinor Wylie, "Atavism," "Wild Peaches"
H.D., "Oread," "Sea Poppies"
Marianne Moore, "To a Snail," "A Grave,"
    "The Fish," "The Paper Nautilus," "The
    Jerboa," "Sea Unicorns and Land Unicorns"
Edna St. Vincent Millay, "The Buck in the
    Snow"
Dorothy Livesay, "Green Rain"
Elizabeth Bishop, "Roosters," "The Fish,"
    "At the Fishhouses," "The Moose"
Denise Levertov, "The Crack"
Ursula Le Guin, "Sur"
Adrienne Rich, "Planetarium," "Power,"
    "Phantasia for Elvira Shatayev"
Sylvia Plath, "The Bee Meeting," "The Arri-
    val of the Bee Box," "Stings," "Win-

tering"
Margaret Atwood, "The Animals in that Coun-
    try," "The Landlady," "Procedures for
    Underground"
Angela Carter, "The Company of Wolves"
Louise Glück, "Horse"


WOMEN AND POLITICS

General Politics:   War and Peace, Oppression
and Slavery

Queen Elizabeth, "The Doubt of Future Foes,"
    "Speech to the Troops at Tilbury"
Elizabeth Barrett Browning, "The Cry of the
    Children," "The Runaway Slave at Pil-
    grim's Point," "Hiram Powers' 'Greek
    Slave,'" "A Curse for a Nation," "Mother
    and Poet"
Frances E.W. Harper, "Aunt Chloe's Politics"
Alice Meynell, "Parentage," "A Father of
    Women," "The Sunderland Children"
Alice Dunbar-Nelson, "I Sit and Sew"
Radclyffe Hall, "Miss Ogilvy Finds Herself"
H.D., "Helen"
Edith Sitwell, "Lullaby," "Serenade:   Any
    Man to Any Woman"
Marianne Moore, "Sojourn in the Whale," "The
    Jerboa," "No Swan So Fine"
Edna St. Vincent Millay, "Apostrophe to Man"
Ruth Pitter, "The Military Harpist"
Elizabeth Bowen, "The Demon Lover"
Stevie Smith, "Lord Barrenstock"
Kay Boyle, "Winter Night"
Lillian Hellman, "Pentimento"
Josephine Miles, "In the town where every
    man is king," "Bureau 2," "Reason," "Why
    We Are Late"
Muriel Rukeyser, "Who in One Lifetime," from
    Letter to the Front
Judith Wright, "To Another Housewife"
Eleanor Ross Taylor, "Welcome Eumenides"
Denise Levertov, "A Note to Olga"

Feminist Politics:    Education and Social
Protest

Margaret Cavendish, _Female Orations_
Lady Mary Chudleigh, "To the Ladies"
Mary Astell, from _A Serious Proposal to the Ladies_
Lady Mary Wortley Montagu, "Letter to the
    Countess of Bute," "Epistle from Mrs.
    Yonge to Her Husband"
Mary Wollstonecraft, from _A Vindication of the Rights of Woman_
Maria Edgeworth, from _Letters to Literary Ladies_
Sojourner Truth, "Ain't I a Woman?," "What
    Time of Night It Is," "Keeping the Thing
    Going . . ."
Elizabeth Barrett Browning, _Aurora Leigh_,
    Book II
Margaret Fuller, from _Woman in the Nineteenth Century_
Elizabeth Cady Stanton, "Address to the New
    York State Legislature, 1860"
Florence Nightingale, from _Cassandra_
Emily Dickinson, 392 ("Through the Dark
    Sod--as Education--"), 401 ("What Soft--
    Cherubic Creatures--"), 593 ("I think I
    was enchanted"), 732 ("She rose to His
    Requirement--dropt"), letter 260
Olive Schreiner, from _Woman and Labour_
Virginia Woolf, "A Woman's College from the
    Outside," "Professions for Women"
Elinor Wylie, "Let No Charitable Hope"
Edna St. Vincent Millay, "To Inez
    Milholland"
Rebecca West, "Indissoluble Matrimony"
Ruth Pitter, "The Irish Patriarch"
Muriel Rukeyser, "More of a Corpse than a
    Woman," "Poem as Mask," "Myth," "Along
    History"
Adrienne Rich, "Snapshots of a Daughter-in-
    Law," "I am in Danger--Sir--," "Planetar-
    ium," "I Dream I'm the Death of Orpheus,"
    "Diving into the Wreck," "Power," from
    _Twenty-One Love Poems_, "Phantasia for
    Elvira Shatayev," "Culture and Anarchy,"
    "When We Dead Awaken"
Lorraine Hansberry, "In Defense of the
    Equality of Men"

Marge Piercy, "The Token Woman," "The
    Friend," "You Don't Understand Me"
Diane Wakoski, "Ringless"
Margaret Atwood, "Rape Fantasies"
Susan Griffin, "I Like to Think of Harriet
    Tubman"


## GENDER AND RACE

Mary Rowlandson, <u>A Narrative of the
    Captivity</u> . . .
Phillis Wheatley, "On Being Brought from
    Africa to America," "To the Right
    Honourable William, Earl of Dartmouth"
Sojourner Truth, "Ain't I a Woman?" "What
    Time of Night It Is,"  "Keeping the Thing
    Going . . ."
Linda Brent, from <u>Incidents in the Life of a
    Slave Girl</u>
Frances E.W. Harper, "Aunt Chloe's Poli-
    tics," "Learning to Read"
Harriet Wilson, from <u>Our Nig</u>
Mourning Dove, from <u>Coyote Tales</u>
Zora Neale Hurston, "Sweat," "How It Feels
    to Be Colored Me"
Lillian Hellman, "Pentimento"
Margaret Walker, "Dark Blood"
Judith Wright, "Half-Caste Girl"
Gwendolyn Brooks, "The Bean Eaters," "We
    Real Cool," "Jessie Mitchell's Mother,"
    "Bronzeville Woman in a Red Hat," "Queen
    of the Blues," from <u>The Womanhood</u>, "Riot"
Nadine Gordimer, "Town and Country Lovers"
Margaret Laurence, "The Loons"
Anne Sexton, "Somewhere in Africa"
Maya Angelou, from <u>I Know Why the Caged Bird
    Sings</u>
Lorraine Hansberry, "In Defense of the
    Equality of Men"
Toni Morrison, <u>The Bluest Eye</u>
Audre Lorde, "Coal," "The House of Yemanjá"
Kamala Das, "An Introduction"
Lucille Clifton, "Admonition"
Toni Cade Bambara, "My Man Bovanne"
Maxine Hong Kingston, "No Name Woman"
Ama Ata Aidoo, "The Message"
Susan Griffin, "I Like to Think of Harriet
    Tubman"

Alice Walker, "Everyday Use," "In Search of
    Our Mothers' Gardens"
Leslie Marmon Silko, "Lullabye"


WOMEN AND WORK

Domesticity and Domestic Service

Anne Bradstreet, from <u>Meditations</u> <u>Divine</u> <u>and</u>
    <u>Moral</u>
Rebecca Cox Jackson, "The Dream of Cakes,"
    "The Dream of Washing Quilts," from <u>Gifts</u>
    <u>of</u> <u>Power</u>
Harriet Beecher Stowe, "The Minister's Housekeepe
Louisa May Alcott, from <u>Work</u>
Alice Dunbar-Nelson, "I Sit and Sew"
Susan Glaspell, "Trifles"
Anna Wickham, "Dedication of the Cook"
Edith Sitwell, "Aubade"
Ruth Pitter, "Old Nelly's Birthday,"
    "Yorkshire Wife's Saga"
Ruth Stone, "In an Iridescent Time,"
    "Absinthe Granny"
Judith Wright, "To Another Housewife"
Maxine Kumin, "Making the Jam Without You"
Anne Sexton, "Housewife"
Edna O'Brien, "A Rose in the Heart"
Toni Morrison, <u>The</u> <u>Bluest</u> <u>Eye</u>
Sylvia Plath, the Bee sequence ("The Bee
    Meeting," "The Arrival of the Bee Box,"
    "Stings," "The Swarm," "Wintering")
Anne Stevenson, "Respectable House"
Alice Walker, "Everyday Use"


Women and Economics

Rebecca Harding Davis, "Life in the Iron-
    Mills"
Sarah Orne Jewett, "The Town Poor"
Dorothy Richardson, "Death"
Virginia Woolf, "Professions for Women"
Katharine Susannah Prichard, "The Cooboo"
Anzia Yezierska, "The Fat of the Land"
Dorothy Parker, "One Perfect Rose"
Meridel Le Sueur, "Annunciation"
Zora Neale Hurston, "Sweat"
Muriel Rukeyser, "Boy with His Hair Cut

Short"
Tillie Olsen, "Tell Me a Riddle"
P.K. Page, "Stenographers," "Typists"
Gwendolyn Brooks, "The Bean Eaters,"
    "Bronzeville Woman in a Red Hat"
Eleanor Ross Taylor, "Welcome Eumenides"
Edna O'Brien, "A Rose in the Heart"
Judy Grahn, "Ella, in a square apron . . .,"
    "Nadine, resting on her neighbor's stoop"


WOMEN AND SPIRITUALITY

Julian of Norwich, from _A_ _Book_ _of_ _Showings_
Margery Kempe, from _The_ _Book_ _of_ _Margery_
    _Kempe_
Anne Bradstreet, "For Deliverance from a
    Fever," and from _Meditations_ _Divine_ _and_
    _Moral_
Jane Lead, from _A_ _Fountain_ _of_ _Gardens_
Mary Rowlandson, from _A_ _Narrative_ _of_ _the_
    _Captivity_ . . .
Rebecca Cox Jackson, from _Gifts_ _of_ _Power_
Emily Brontë, "The Prisoner," "No coward
    soul is mine,"
Emily Dickinson, 271 ("A solemn thing--it
    was--I said--"), 365 ("Dare you see a
    Soul _at_ _the_ _White_ _Heat?_"), 384 ("No Rack
    can torture me--"), 528 ("Mine--by the
    Right of the White Election!"), 722
    ("Sweet Mountains--Ye tell Me no lie--"),
    792 ("Through the strait pass of
    suffering"), 1072 ("Title divine--is
    mine!"), 1651 ("A Word made Flesh is
    seldom"), 1657 ("Eden is that old-
    fashioned House")
Christina Rossetti, "Symbols," "A Soul,"
    "The World," "Shut Out," "Up-Hill," "The
    Convent Threshold"
Olive Schreiner, "A Little African Story"
H.D., from _Tribute_ _to_ _the_ _Angels_
Denise Levertov, "The Wings"
Anne Sexton, "Consorting with Angels," from
    "O Ye Tongues"
Lucille Clifton, "anna speaks," "mary's
    dream," "how he . . .," "holy night,"
    "song of mary," "island mary"

WOMEN AND MADNESS

Anne Finch, "The Spleen"
Elizabeth Barrett Browning, "A True Dream,"
    "Grief"
Charlotte Brontë, _Jane Eyre_
George Eliot, "The Lifted Veil"
Emily Dickinson, 280 ("I Felt a Funeral, in
    my Brain"), 327 ("Before I got my eye put
    out"), 425 ("Good Morning--Midnight--"),
    435 ("Much Madness is divinest Sense--"),
    462 ("Why make it doubt--it hurts it
    so--"), 510 ("It was not Death, for I
    stood up"), 512 ("The Soul has Bandaged
    moments--"), 579 ("I had been hungry, all
    the years--"), 593 ("I think I was en-
    chanted"), 601 ("A still--Volcano--
    Life--"), 642 ("Me from Myself--to ba-
    nish--"), 670 ("One need not be a
    Chamber--to be Haunted--"), 959 ("A loss
    of something ever felt I--"), 1705 ("Vol-
    canoes be in Sicily"), letters 233, 248
Christina Rossetti, "Cobwebs," "The Convent
    Threshold," "Goblin Market"
Alice James, from the _Diary_
Charlotte Perkins Gilman, "The Yellow
    Wallpaper"
Mary Elizabeth Coleridge, "The Other Side of
    the Mirror," "Doubt"
Charlotte Mew, "The Quiet House"
Ellen Glasgow, "Jordan's End"
Virginia Woolf, "Shakespeare's Sister" (from
    _A Room of One's Own_)
Susan Glaspell, "Trifles"
Katharine Susannah Prichard, "The Cooboo"
Katherine Mansfield, "The Daughters of the
    Late Colonel"
Mourning Dove, "Coyote Kills Owl-Woman"
Djuna Barnes, "Cassation"
Louise Bogan, "Evening in the Sanitarium"
Tillie Olsen, "Tell Me a Riddle"
Margaret Walker, "Mollie Means"
Doris Lessing, "To Room 19"
May Swenson, "Bleeding"
Gwendolyn Brooks, "The Crazy Woman"
Eleanor Ross Taylor, "Welcome Eumenides"
Denise Levertov, "In Mind"
Anne Sexton, "Her Kind"
Adrienne Rich, "Power"

Toni Morrison, _The Bluest Eye_
Sylvia Plath, "The Disquieting Muses," "Lady
    Lazarus," "Ariel," "Medusa," "Daddy,"
    "Edge"
Louise Glück, "Dedication to Hunger"
Maxine Hong Kingston, "No Name Woman"


WOMEN AND VIOLENCE

Mary Rowlandson, from _A Narrative of the
    Captivity_ . . .
Rebecca Cox Jackson, "A Dream of Slaughter"
Elizabeth Barrett Browning, "The Runaway
    Slave at Pilgrim's Point," "Mother and
    Poet"
Charlotte Brontë, _Jane Eyre_
Emily Brontë, "The Prisoner"
George Eliot, "The Lifted Veil"
Harriet Wilson, from _Our Nig_
Emily Dickinson, 512 ("The Soul has Bandaged
    moments--"), 754 ("My Life had stood--a
    Loaded Gun--")
Christina Rossetti, "Goblin Market"
Mary E. Wilkins Freeman, "Old Woman Magoun"
Augusta Gregory, "Spreading the News"
Olive Schreiner, "A Little African Story"
Charlotte Perkins Gilman, "The Yellow
    Wallpaper"
Mary Elizabeth Coleridge, "The Other Side of
    a Mirror"
Susan Glaspell, "Trifles"
Katharine Susannah Prichard, "The Cooboo"
Elinor Wylie, "Atavism"
Mourning Dove, "Coyote Kills Owl-Woman"
Rebecca West, "Indissoluble Matrimony"
Dorothy Parker, "Résumé"
Louise Bogan, "The Dream"
Elizabeth Bowen, "The Demon Lover"
Zora Neale Hurston, "Sweat"
Margaret Walker, "Molly Means," "Kissie Lee"
Gwendolyn Brooks, "Riot"
Shirley Jackson, "The Lottery"
May Swenson, "Bleeding"
Flannery O'Connor, "Good Country People"
Toni Morrison, _The Bluest Eye_
Sylvia Plath, "Daddy," "Lady Lazarus"
Joyce Carol Oates, "Where Are You
    Going? . . ."

Margaret Atwood, "[You Fit into Me]," "Rape
    Fantasies"
Angela Carter, "The Company of Wolves"
Maxine Hong Kingston, "No Name Woman"


FEMALE COMMUNITIES

Mary Astell, from A Serious Proposal to the
    Ladies
Elizabeth Gaskell, from Cranford
Emily Dickinson, 24 ("There is a morn by men
    unseen--"), 722 ("Sweet Mountains--Ye
    tell Me no lie--")
Lady Augusta Gregory, "Spreading the News"
Mary Elizabeth Coleridge, "Regina," "The
    White Women," "Day-Dream"
Susan Glaspell, "Trifles"
Virginia Woolf, "A Woman's College from the
    Outside"
Isak Dinesen, "The Blank Page"
Ursula Le Guin, "Sur"
Adrienne Rich, "Phantasia for Elvira
    Shatayev"
Audre Lorde, "The Women of Dan"
Joanna Russ, "When It Changed"


WOMEN ON SPECIFIC WOMEN

Mary Sidney Herbert, "To the Thrice Sacred
    Queen Elizabeth"
Anne Bradstreet, "In Honour of that High and
    Mighty Princess"
Katherine Philips, "To My Excellent
    Lucasia. . ."
Anne Finch, "Friendship between Ephelia and
    Ardelia," "The Circuit of Apollo"
Elizabeth Barrett Browning, "To George Sand:
    A Desire," "To George Sand: A Recogni-
    tion"
Emily Dickinson, 312 ("Her--'last
    Poems'--"), 593 ("I think I was enchant-
    ed"), 1562 ("Her Losses make our Gains
    ashamed--")
Christina Rossetti, "Enrica, 1865"
Amy Lowell, "The Sisters"
Virginia Woolf, "Jane Eyre and Wuthering
    Heights"

Dorothy Parker, "Harriet Beecher Stowe,"
    "George Sand"
Anaïs Nin, <u>Diary</u> entry on June Miller
Dorothy Livesay, "The Three Emily's"
Elizabeth Bishop, "Invitation to Miss
    Marianne Moore"
May Sarton, "My Sisters, O My Sisters,"
    "Letter from Chicago"
Muriel Rukeyser, "Käthe Kollwitz"
Eleanor Ross Taylor, "Welcome Eumenides"
Denise Levertov, "A Note to Olga"
Carolyn Kizer, from "Pro Femina"
Maxine Kumin, "How It Is"
Anne Sexton, "Sylvia's Death"
Adrienne Rich, "I Am in Danger--Sir--,"
    "Power," "Planetarium," "Phantasia for
    Elvira Shatayev," "Culture and Anarchy"
Anne Stevenson, "Rereading Jane"
Diane Wakoski, "My Trouble"
Erica Jong, "Alcestis on the Poetry Circuit"
Susan Griffin, "I Like to Think of Harriet
    Tubman"
Alice Walker, "In Search of Our Mothers'
    Gardens"


MYTHS OF FEMALENESS

Amelia Lanier, "Eve's Apology in Defense of
    Women"
Mary Wollstonecraft, <u>A Vindication of the
    Rights of Woman</u>, Chapter II
Elizabeth Barrett Browning, from Book I,
    <u>Aurora Leigh</u>
Frances E.W. Harper, "Vashti"
Christina Rossetti, "Eve," "Venus's Looking-
    Glass"
Mary Elizabeth Coleridge, "Regina," "The
    Witch," "The White Women," "Day-Dream"
Willa Cather, "Coming, Aphrodite!"
Amy Lowell, "Madonna of the Evening
    Flowers," "Venus Transiens"
H.D., "Oread," "Euridice," "Helen," from
    <u>Tribute to the Angels</u>
Edith Sitwell, "A Bird's Song," "Song"
    ("Where is all the bright company gone")
Marianne Moore, "Marriage"
Mourning Dove, "Coyote Kills Owl-Woman"
Edna St. Vincent Millay, "Oh, sleep forever

in the Latmian cave," "An Ancient Ges-
ture"
Louise Bogan, "Medusa," "Cassandra"
Stevie Smith, "How Cruel Is the Story of
Eve"
Kathleen Raine, "Isis Wanderer," "Kore in
Hades," "What Substance Had Euridice,"
"On Its Way I See"
Dorothy Livesay, "Eve"
May Sarton, "The Muse as Medusa"
Muriel Rukeyser, "The Birth of Venus," "The
Poem as Mask," "Myth"
Judith Wright, "Ishtar," "Eve to Her
Daughters"
Denise Levertov, "The Goddess," "Song for
Ishtar," "Eros at Temple Stream," "Abel's
Bride"
Carolyn Kizer, "Semele Recycled"
Anne Sexton, "Her Kind," "Somewhere in
Africa"
Adrienne Rich, "I Dream I'm the Death of
Orpheus," "Planetarium," "Diving into the
Wreck"
Sylvia Plath, "Medusa," "The Disquieting
Muses," "Lady Lazarus"
Margaret Atwood, from _Circe/Mud_ _Poems_


WOMEN AND CREATIVITY

Anne Bradstreet, "The Prologue," "The Author
to Her Book"
Anne Killigrew, "Upon the Saying that My
Verses . . ."
Anne Finch, "The Introduction," "The Circuit
of Apollo," "The Answer"
Fanny Burney, from the _Diary_
Mary Wollstonecraft, Chapter XIII of _A_ _Vin-_
_dication_
Maria Edgeworth, from _Letters_ _to_ _Literary_
_Ladies_
Elizabeth Barrett Browning, "A True Dream,"
"To George Sand: A Desire" and "A Recog-
nition," excerpts from Books II and IV of
_Aurora_ _Leigh_, "Mother and Poet"
Margaret Fuller, "[Muse and Minerva]" in
_Woman_ _in_ _the_ _Nineteenth_ _Century_
Emily Brontë, "The Night-Wind," "Aye, there
it is! . . .," "A Day Dream"

Emily Dickinson, 271 ("A solemn thing--it
    was--I said--"), 288 ("I'm Nobody!  Who
    are you?"), 312 ("Her--'Last Poems'--"),
    365 ("Dare you see a Soul <u>at</u> <u>the</u> <u>White</u>
    <u>Heat</u>?"), 441 ("This is my letter to the
    World" ), ("I'm ceded--I've stopped being
    Theirs--"), 528 ("Mine--by the Right of
    the White Election!"), 569 ("I reckon--
    when I count at all--"), 593 ("I think I
    was enchanted"), 613 ("They shut me up in
    Prose--"), 657 ("I dwell in Possibil-
    ity--"),  669 ("No Romance sold unto"),
    709 ("Publication--is the Auction"), 1072
    ("Title divine--is mine"), 1129 ("Tell
    all the Truth but tell it slant--"), 1138
    ("A Spider sewed at Night"), 1651 ("A
    Word made Flesh is seldom"), letters 260,
    261, 263, 268
Christina Rossetti, "A Soul," "Shut Out,"
    "Goblin Market," "In an Artist's Studio"
Kate Chopin, <u>The</u> <u>Awakening</u>
Charlotte Perkins Gilman, "The Yellow
    Wallpaper"
Edith Wharton, "The Angel at the Grave"
Willa Cather, "Coming, Aphrodite!"
Amy Lowell, "The Sisters"
Gertrude Stein, "Picasso," "Ada"
Anna Hempstead Branch, from <u>Sonnets</u> <u>from</u> <u>a</u>
    <u>Lock</u> <u>Box</u>
Virginia Woolf, "<u>Jane</u> <u>Eyre</u> and <u>Wuthering</u>
    <u>Heights</u>," from <u>A</u> <u>Room</u> <u>of</u> <u>One's</u> <u>Own</u>, "Pro-
    fessions for Women"
Isak Dinesen, "The Blank Page"
H.D., "Fragment 36," from <u>Tribute</u> <u>to</u> <u>the</u>
    <u>Angels</u>
Marianne Moore, "To a Snail," "Poetry," "No
    Swan So Fine," "An Egyptian Pulled Glass
    Bottle in the Shape of a Fish," "His
    Shield"
Dorothy Parker, from "A Pig's Eye View of
    Literature"
Louise Bogan, "Several Voices out of a
    Cloud," "The Dream"
Ruth Pitter, "The Military Harpist"
Stevie Smith, "Souvenir de Monsieur Poop"
Anaïs Nin, <u>Diary</u> entry on [Gender and
    Creativity]
Elizabeth Bishop, "The Man-Moth," "One
    Art," "Pink Dog"

May Sarton, "My Sisters, O My Sisters,"
    "Letter from Chicago," "The Muse as
    Medusa"
Muriel Rukeyser, "The Poem as Mask"
Judith Wright, "Request to a Year"
Carson McCullers, "Wunderkind"
Gwendolyn Brooks, "The Crazy Woman," "Queen
    of the Blues"
Muriel Spark, "The Fathers' Daughters"
Carolyn Kizer, from "Pro Femina"
Anne Sexton, "Sylvia's Death," "In Celebra-
    tion of My Uterus," from "O Ye Tongues"
Adrienne Rich, "I Am in Danger--Sir--,"
    "Culture and Anarchy," "Power," "When We
    Dead Awaken"
Sylvia Plath, "The Colossus," "The Disquiet-
    ing Muses," "Stings," "Words"
Kamala Das, "An Introduction"
Margaret Atwood, from <u>Circe/Mud</u> <u>Poems</u>
Erica Jong, "Alcestis on the Poetry Cir-
    cuit," "Castration of the Pen"
Alice Walker, "In Search of Our Mothers'
    Gardens"

# 5

## ENRICHING STANDARD SURVEY, INTRODUCTORY, AND PERIOD COURSES

Many teachers of standard survey, introductory, and period courses in British and American literature have, at one time or another, expressed an interest in expanding the scope of the materials they cover in their classes. Until now, however, instructors concerned to familiarize their students with the female literary tradition in English have only been able to supplement asignments of "mainstream" male-authored texts in an ad hoc, catch-as-catch-can fashion, ordering individual novels and collections of verse or fiction or else offering readings in anthologies limited to a single genre (poetry, drama, science fiction) or theme ("Images of Women"). We hope that the publication of NALW will help change this situation, allowing teachers to undertake more systematic procedures of enrichment.

Traditional undergraduate survey courses in English or American literature ("Beowulf through Yeats," "Winthrop through Hemingway") might well be the first targets for such enrichment. Instructors wishing to offer a more complex and sophisticated view of the literary tradition in English than the vision that is usually proposed in standard anthologies might well decide to assign NALW as a supplement to another collection. An advantage of such a move is that it need only be made once; in other words, groups of teachers (or directors of undergraduate studies and department heads) who choose to coordinate their surveys of English and American literature could arrange to have students purchase NALW at the beginning of a survey series for use throughout the entire sequence of courses, since this one volume covers both British and American literature by women from the earliest periods to the present.

How, specifically, might instructors use NALW to supplement a traditional survey course? To begin with, when providing introductory overviews of such concepts as periodization and genre, they might set the periods and genres covered in our anthology against those defined in other anthologies in order to demonstrate the discrepancies between one literary history and another.  As the title of a section in an important essay by the historian Joan Kelly suggests ("Did Women Have a Renaissance?"), a narrative of female cultural triumphs and defeats might be very different from the "mainstream" story of male cultural evolution that we all learned in school.  Students ought, of course, to learn the traditional history, but they should also learn that, though it has heretofore functioned as in some sense normative, it is not the only story. Readings of the period introductions in NALW along with the period introductions in other anthologies would surely help to dramatize this point.  In addition, a simple scrutiny of the tables of contents presented in the various anthologies would probably clarify the issues associated with historical analysis, canon formation, and generic evaluation.

The question of generic evaluation is, of course, a trans-historical one; such genres as the novel, the verse-drama, and the ode can be detached from their sociocultural contexts and studied structurally, in and for themselves.  At the same time, however, as our discussion of "Gender and Genre" in this manual suggests, both the development and the valorization (or devaluation) of certain genres have been deeply associated with the differing relationships between tradition and the male or female talent.  Teachers interested in the historical conditions that fostered, for instance, the rise of the novel might therefore pair selections in NALW with the texts in, say, The Norton Anthology of English Literature, to demonstrate the wider range of prose and verse forms available to male authors; then, after discussing the reasons (e.g., education, cultural authority) why men of letters had access to such a range of genres, these teachers might show how the development in the eighteenth century of a middle-class female audience of novel readers facilitated female authorship of novels along with what sometimes seemed to be a general cultural devaluation of novel-reading and novel-writing as secondary, "effeminate" activi-

ties.   Similarly, instructors interested in tracing the history of, say, the verse-drama or the
ode might want to consider the conditions that
prevented such hypothetical women as Woolf's
Judith Shakespeare or such real women as Mary
Sidney Herbert from working extensively in these
forms.

After examining such general issues as the
dissonance between male and female periodization
or the discrepancy between male and female generic practices, however, teachers would surely
want to use specific texts in NALW to enrich and
illuminate the literary history they explore with
their students.  Such a use of the anthology
would, of course, elaborate and support general
points about periodization and genre, but it
would also offer a set of significantly new perspectives on "mainstream" themes and topics.  To
facilitate understanding of these perspectives
and of the gender differences which led to intellectual and aesthetic differences, instructors
could probably employ at least three distinct
strategies: (1) most obviously (and generally)
they might decide to assign a representative
range of works by women in the traditional period
they are teaching in a class; (2) more specifically, they might assign female-authored texts,
from a particular period, that are thematically
or topically related to the "mainstream" texts
they have assigned from that period; and (3) most
specifically, they might pair works by individual
female and male writers who have significant
historical, generic, or thematic connections.

The first of these strategies would of
course be a simple one to pursue, particularly in
courses focusing on English or American literature from the eighteenth century to the present--
periods for which NALW includes a number of
important but heretofore largely untaught texts
whose availability may significantly alter our
sense of the "teachable" canon.  Instructors
directing a survey of nineteenth- and twentieth-
century British literature, for example, could
easily construct a syllabus which would draw upon
works by, say, Maria Edgeworth, Jane Austen,
Elizabeth Gaskell, Charlotte Brontë, Florence
Nightingale, Alice Meynell, Lady Gregory, Olive
Schreiner, Mary Elizabeth Coleridge, Charlotte
Mew, Dorothy Richardson, Anna Wickham, Edith

Sitwell, Rebecca West, Jean Rhys, and Ruth Pitter
(none of whom is represented in most standard
British surveys) along with selections by male
writers from Wordsworth through Yeats; in addition, they could supplement a standard anthology's offerings of texts by Dorothy Wordsworth,
Mary Shelley, Elizabeth Barrett Browning, Emily
Brontë, George Eliot, Christina Rossetti, Virginia Woolf, and Katherine Mansfield with readings
drawn from NALW.

The second strategy would probably be almost
as easy to implement.  In covering such topics as
the Romantic concepts of Nature and Imagination,
for instance, it might be fruitful to supplement
texts by Wordsworth, Coleridge, Shelley, and
Keats with writings by Dorothy Wordsworth, Mary
Shelley, Elizabeth Barrett Browning, and the
Brontës.  Similarly, in dealing with the Victorian imperative to "Work while it is called today, for the night cometh wherein no man can
work," it might be interesting to cluster texts
by Carlyle, Tennyson, Browning, and Arnold with
selections by Elizabeth Barrett Browning, Charlotte Brontë, George Eliot, Florence Nightingale,
and Olive Schreiner.  Finally, in approaching
such a subject as modernism, it might be helpful
to read works by Yeats, Lawrence, Joyce, and
Eliot along with writings by Dorothy Richardson,
Gertrude Stein, Virginia Woolf, Katherine Mansfield, and Edith Sitwell.

For instructors who teach surveys which
focus--as many do--on a carefully limited and
defined set of major authors, the third strategy
mentioned above would no doubt be the most appropriate.  If we continue for a moment to explore a
hypothetical course in nineteenth- and twentieth-
century British literature, for instance, obvious
pairs to consider studying would be such sets of
relatives, friends, or rivals as Dorothy and
William Wordsworth, Percy and Mary Shelley, Elizabeth Barrett and Robert Browning, Christina and
Dante Gabriel Rossetti, Lady Gregory and W. B.
Yeats, Virginia Woolf and James Joyce, Katherine
Mansfield and D. H. Lawrence.  In earlier periods
of British literature, similar pairs might include Mary Sidney Herbert and Philip Sidney,
Aphra Behn and John Wilmot, Earl of Rochester,
Anne Finch and Alexander Pope, Mary Wollstone-
craft and William Godwin.  In American litera-

ture, such pairs might include Anne Bradstreet
and Edward Taylor, Margaret Fuller and Ralph
Waldo Emerson (or Nathaniel Hawthorne), Linda
Brent and Frederick Douglass, Emily Dickinson and
Walt Whitman, Alice James and Henry (or William)
James (or Edith Wharton and Henry James), H.D.
and Ezra Pound, Marianne Moore and Wallace
Stevens, Zora Neale Hurston and Langston Hughes,
Sylvia Plath and Robert Lowell, Audre Lorde and
Imamu Amiri Baraka.

Pairings of female and male authors need
not, however, be based simply on consanguinity or
contemporaneity.  Rather, they can be derived
from finer definitions of the thematic issues
mentioned above.  For example, if we go back yet
once more to our proposed course in nineteenth-
and twentieth-century British literature, we can
see that it might be possible to pair writers who
address common topics or create similar images,
even when those artists stand to each other as
precursor and descendant rather than as contemporaries.  Byron and Charlotte Brontë, after all,
both depict similarly defiant and often alienated
protagonists, so that it might be fascinating to
read selected cantos from, say, <u>Childe</u> <u>Harold</u>
along with <u>Jane</u> <u>Eyre</u>, studying not only Rochester
but also Jane as types of the "Byronic hero" who
stalks "apart . . . in joyless revery."  In the
same way, looking at turn-of-the-century American
literature, it might be useful to pair regional-
ists like Mark Twain and Sarah Orne Jewett or
Bret Harte and Mary Wilkins Freeman in order to
consider the similarities and differences between
male and female strategies of mimesis, critiques
of culture, and fantasies of freedom.

Finally, besides using <u>NALW</u> to investigate
issues of periodization and genre evaluation and
to explore the relationships between female and
male literary histories, an instructor interested
in the questions raised by "national" literatures
might use this volume--which is unique in its
crossing of geographic boundaries to include
works by English, Irish, American, Canadian,
Australian, and other English-speaking authors--
as part of an effort to define the connections
(and disparities) between, say, nineteenth-
century American literature and nineteenth-century English literature or to explore the ways in
which writers from such previously colonized

countries as Canada, Australia, India, New Zea-
land, South Africa, and Ghana resist and revise
the hegemonic English traditions they have inherited from their former rulers.

   In the first case, the fact that our table
of contents juxtaposes works by Sojourner Truth,
Elizabeth Barrett Browning, Margaret Fuller,
Elizabeth Gaskell, Harriet Beecher Stowe, Elizabeth Cady Stanton, and Charlotte Brontë suggests
relationships among Victorian industrialization,
American abolitionism, and trans-Atlantic feminism that are not usually explored in survey
courses.  In the second case, the fact that our
table of contents includes texts by such authors
from emergent nations as Margaret Laurence, Alice
Munro, Dorothy Livesay, P.K. Page, H. H. Richardson, Susannah Prichard, Margaret Atwood, Nadine
Gordimer, Kamala Das, and Ama Ata Aidoo drama-
tizes the existence of a tradition not ordinarily
examined in survey courses--a strong and self-
defining strain of English literature that has
roots in the English language even while it quite
consciously sets itself in some sense against the
supposedly central traditions of England and the
United States.

   NALW can also, of course, be used as either
a centerpiece or a supplement in many "mainstream" courses besides conventional undergraduate surveys.  Faculty members at women's col-
leges who teach courses such as "Introduction to
Literature" (focusing either on one or several
genres) might well decide to convey interpretive
skills through the analysis of a body of material
that would have distinctly personal relevance to
their student bodies.  Similarly, faculty members
at larger, coeducational institutions might want
to adopt the book as a text for theme-oriented
undergraduate courses in composition or literary
interpretation.  The anthology could be assigned,
for example--with or without supplementation--in
lower-division classes centered on such topics as
"Growing Up Female" or "Women and Politics."  In
addition, the volume could easily be used as a
text for introductory courses in poetry and short
fiction.  Finally, NALW could be ordered as an
enrichment text for traditional classes in specific periods, particularly for classes in nine-
teenth- or twentieth-century American and British
literature.  Perhaps, indeed, it is not exces-

sively utopian for us to hope that there will
even be some instructors of, for example, Victorian literature who choose to use <u>NALW</u> as their
central anthology, supplementing the book as
necessary by ordering a few male-authored works
like <u>Sartor</u> <u>Resartus</u> and <u>Great</u> <u>Expectations</u> in
order to offer their students a "different" per-
spective on the spirit of the age.

6

## ESSAY QUESTIONS AND RESEARCH TOPICS

Because <u>NALW</u> can be used as a textbook in many different kinds of courses, there are a number of approaches the instructor can take to written assignments. This section on essay questions and research topics is therefore organized into five major areas:

1. Assignments related to the interpretation of individual texts and authors

2. Questions focused on generic issues

3. Study topics associated with thematic connections between texts

4. Research problems centered on women's studies issues

5. Questions dealing with the relationship between male and female literary history

## INTERPRETATION OF INDIVIDUAL TEXTS AND AUTHORS

A surprising number of the works in <u>NALW</u> have not yet received much critical attention. Undergraduates can be asked to present close readings of poems and prose narratives that will be, for the first time, illuminated by analyses of such formal considerations as speaker, structure, image pattern, and allusive framework as well as by examinations of such stylistic techniques as line length, rhythm, rhyme, diction, word order, repetition, and parallelism. The following questions are meant to suggest representative assignments that would elicit critical studies of the ways in which texts establish significance.

1. Sometimes the best way to capture the style of a given writer is to imitate or parody one of her works. Some teachers may want to ask

students to produce imitations or parodies of those stylists whose work is most idiosyncratic.

2. Why does an author choose a particular point of view and how does she realize it? Students might be asked to explore the counterpointed speakers in Margaret Cavendish's "Female Orations," the choice of a poetic persona like Aunt Chloe in Frances E.W. Harper's "Aunt Chloe's Politics," the ironic narrative voice of an Edith Wharton story, or the juxtaposition of third- and first-person perspectives in The Bluest Eye.

3. How and why does an author choose to create characters who function as antagonists, foils, or doubles? The two male speakers of Maria Edgeworth's Letters to Literary Ladies are opponents on the subject of female creativity, but can they be said to share certain assumptions? How do marital conflicts in either "The Mortal Immortal" or "The Lifted Veil" serve to associate women with the body and men with the mind? What is the relationship between Emily Dickinson, as she presents herself in her poems and letters, and the Master she invokes? Those teachers who have explored the doubling of Jane Eyre and Bertha Mason Rochester in Charlotte Brontë's novel may want to ask students to analyze the dialectical relationship of or the doubling of characters in other works.

4. How and why does an author evoke a particular setting? It would be possible to trace women's obsession with spatial confinement, and specifically with the confines of the house, from Anne Finch's protest against servile housekeeping to Bertha Mason Rochester's and Linda Brent's confinements in the attics to Alice James's flight into a sickroom and the escape of Doris Lessing's heroine into "Room 19," the only room of her own she can find. Just as interesting, students might be asked to consider how a writer creates a particular societal milieu: Fanny Burney's London, Willa Cather's Greenwich Village, and Anaïs Nin's Paris all furnish different perspectives on the city, while Dorothy Wordsworth's Grasmere Journals, Sarah Orne Jewett's New England stories, and Zora Neale Hurston's Southern tales all provide different visions of the country.

5. Why does a writer choose to present interpolated stories or framing narratives? It

might be especially interesting to examine the
relationship between frame and inner story in
Isak Dinesen's "The Blank Page" or Kay Boyle's
"Winter Night."  In addition, the three novels
included in NALW use interpolated stories that
can be analyzed in relation to the main plots of
these works, while similar studies can be made of
such long stories as "Coming, Aphrodite!" and
"Tell Me a Riddle."

6.  Regional and ethnic writers sometimes
try to capture certain cultural traits by using
colloquialisms.  How do such writers as Sarah
Orne Jewett, Anzia Yezierska, Zora Neale Hurston,
Margaret Walker, and Ama Ata Aidoo represent the
unique intonations of a dialect and to what
effect?

7.  Sometimes a title provides a clue to the
symbolic structure in a book.  Students could be
asked to trace the significance of "awakening,"
as it relates to sleeping, dreaming, fantasizing,
and waking in Kate Chopin's The Awakening.  Similarly, students might analyze the classical reference in the title of Eleanor Ross Taylor's
"Welcome Eumenides" or the reference to Matthew
Arnold that constitutes the title of Adrienne
Rich's "Culture and Anarchy."

8.  Why and how does an author integrate
quotations or allusions into a text?  Marianne
Moore's "Marriage," perhaps the most difficult
poem included in NALW, could be approached
through a study of Moore's own footnotes and of
the ways in which they function for the reader.
But students could also explore the function of
allusion in long poems from Amelia Lanier's
"Eve's Apology in Defense of Women" to Margaret
Atwood's Circe/Mud Poems.

9.  What are the uniquely visual or auditory
techniques certain poets use?  From Emily Dickinson's dashes to May Swenson's "concrete" line
placements and caesuras, from Anne Finch's quasi-
heroic couplets to Dorothy Parker's neat rhymes,
the poems in NALW can be approached by asking
students to explore how the look and sound of a
particular verse relate to the overall effect
that text achieves.

10.  Students can be asked to trace a particular line of development in the work of those
individual writers who are most amply represented
in NALW.  The intellectual and aesthetic evolu-

tion of contemporary poets (for instance, Sylvia
Plath or Adrienne Rich) can be studied in the
selections included in the anthology, as can the
growth of major nineteenth-century poets (e.g.,
Dickinson, Rossetti, and Emily Brontë). Those
students interested in investigating the literary
evolution of short-story writers or novelists,
moreover, could write papers based on outside
reading in individual oeuvres.

11. Many students may want to research the
lives of particular writers. There are a number
of women (especially in the first two sections of
NALW) who have not yet been the subjects of
definitive biographies; however, most of the
major authors from the nineteenth century on have
received some scholarly attention. When possible, the best biographies of these figures are
mentioned in NALW's headnotes or in its bibliography. From Charlotte Brontë's experience of
her older sisters' death at boarding school to
Elizabeth Barrett Browning's and Margaret Fuller's involvement in Italian politics, George
Eliot's tangled relationship with her brother and
Edith Wharton's divorce, the lives of women writers can be used to illuminate the work represented in the anthology. In addition, it might
be interesting to ask students to examine dis-
junctions between an individual's life and her
work: Jane Austen, for example, never married,
but all of her heroines are bent upon just that
fate. Similarly, Sylvia Plath was not a Jew, but
she uses metaphors of the Holocaust extensively.
Both Alice Walker and Toni Cade Bambara present
themselves in essays and interviews as black
militants, yet their fiction often seems to crit-
icize political radicalism. Students might be
asked how one can account for such dissonances.

12. Some teachers might want to ask students to view the movies and listen to the re-
cordings of contemporary writers. There are
filmed interviews with Brooks, Sexton, Levertov,
and Welty, among others, as well as fine films
about certain authors (for instance, Gertrude
Stein in "When This You See, Remember Me"), re-
cordings (of, say, Sylvia Plath reading her own
work), and dramatizations (of stories by, for
example, O'Connor). Students might be asked to
discuss how the self-presentation of a writer or
the dramatization of her work contradicts or

extends their understanding of the texts they
have read.


GENERIC QUESTIONS

Using the generic tables in this guide, a
teacher can ask students to explore the transformation of a particular mode of writing as it
evolved through the six historical periods represented in NALW. There are a number of genres,
moreover, that we did not include in our tables,
genres that may be of interest to individual
students. Although we excluded lists of, for
example, "elegies" or "mortuary verse," because
those genres did not seem central to enough women
writers, students may want to consider how and
why a particular author was drawn to such a form.
For the most part, however, the questions that
follow pertain to those genres that we have re-
viewed in the third section of this guide.

1.  Any of the genres in NALW can serve as a
model for student writing. Students might be
asked to produce a sonnet, a dramatic monologue,
a diary entry, a regional sketch, or a Gothic
tale. Just as interestingly, students might be
asked to write an "extra" chapter for any of the
three novels included in NALW.
2.  Sometimes students can learn a great
deal about form by "translating" a story into a
one-act play, or a long poem into a short story.
Similarly, they can rewrite a comic story in a
tragic mode, or vice versa. In any of these
cases, an assignment in creative writing might be
accompanied by either a written or an oral analysis of how the adaptation illuminated the conventions of a particular form.
3.  It may make sense to ask students to
pair two works written in the same mode in order
to explore the use of similar or different
aesthetic strategies. If instructors wish to
emphasize the historical transformations of literary conventions, they may ask students to compare some of Elizabeth Barrett Browning's sonnets
with sonnets by Anna Hempstead Branch or Edna St.
Vincent Millay. If teachers are interested in
recurrent motifs, they may pair Elizabeth Bowen's
"The Demon Lover" and Joyce Carol Oates' "Where

Are You Going, Where Have You Been?," encouraging
students to explore the ways in which both stories blend realistic detail with supernatural
elements to describe women who are literally
swept away.

4. When teaching either Lady Augusta
Gregory's "Spreading the News" or Susan Glaspell's "Trifles," instructors may find that students are unfamiliar with theatrical conventions.
After discussing the play as a script, such
teachers could explore the functions of the
director and the actor, asking students either to
perform sections of a play or to write about one
character from a technical perspective: what
movements, gestures, intonations, facial expressions, costumes, and pacing might directors or
actors choose in order best to stage a particular
scene?

5. Certain genres seem especially important
to women writers. Students might explore "confessional" verse or regional fiction from this
point of view, or, more generally, they might
analyze the importance of narrative poetry to
women poets. Similarly, those teachers who are
using all three novels in <u>NALW</u> could ask students
to consider the significance of women's contributions to the history of prose narrative. More
specifically, some students might be interested
in examining women's contributions to fantasy and
science fiction. After reading, for instance,
Joanna Russ's "What Can a Heroine Do?" (in Susan
Koppelman Cornillon's <u>Images of Women in Fic-
tion</u>), such students could speculate on the ways
in which fantasy in general and science fiction
in particular liberate women writers from the
constraints imposed by so-called "realism."

6. Besides containing prose and journal
entries, <u>NALW</u> includes some epistolary verse.
Teachers might ask students to explore the use of
the letter form in poems from Anne Bradstreet's
"A Letter to Her Husband" to May Sarton's "Letter
from Chicago."

7. The essays in <u>NALW</u> can be studied in
terms of their employment of argumentative, narrative, poetic, or dramatic strategies. Student
essays can trace the imagistic movement of, say,
Fuller's prose or the dramatic techniques employed by, for example, Woolf's essays.

8. The three novels in <u>NALW</u> present almost

unlimited opportunities for assignments that draw
on generic issues.  Each can be analyzed separately or all can be considered together as forms
of the female Bildungsroman.  In addition, each
of the three novels poses particular generic
questions.  How and why does Charlotte Brontë
draw on Gothic material in Jane Eyre?  How does
Kate Chopin exploit realistic details for symbolic purposes, and to what extent does she construct The Awakening as a kind of fin de siècle
fantasy?  How do the dramatic monologues work in
The Bluest Eye, and why does Morrison alternate
them with more conventionally "realistic" modes
of narration?

9.  The forms and diction of children's
literature are employed in very different ways by
Christina Rossetti, Ruth Stone, Sylvia Plath,
Angela Carter, Toni Morrison, and many other
writers in NALW.  Students can explore these
authors' use of nursery rhymes and fairy tales
in, for example, "Goblin Market," "The Song of
Absinthe Granny," "Daddy," "The Company of
Wolves," and The Bluest Eye.

10.  Although letters, diaries, journals,
and autobiographies share an impulse that can be
said to be directly confessional, their formal
strategies and effects can be quite different,
and that difference could be the subject of student papers.

11.  When a writer has moved from one genre
or style to another during the course of her
career, the critic can try to explain what made
this development possible and what significance
it has in the evolution of a given oeuvre.  H.D.,
for example, is represented in NALW by the short
Imagistic lyrics she wrote early in her career
and by long excerpts from Tribute to the Angels
which demonstrate the emergence of her later
interest in the extended narrative poem.  In an
equally notable stylistic transformation, Gertrude Stein turned away from the traditional plot
that can still be glimpsed in her early "The
Gentle Lena" and moved increasingly toward the
experimental portraits typified by "Picasso" and
"Ada."  Students might want to analyze both the
continuities and the discontinuities implicit in
such striking generic or stylistic shifts.

THEMATIC QUESTIONS

Using the thematic tables in this manual, a teacher can ask students to compare and contrast different writers' presentations of central subjects and issues in the female literary tradition. Most obviously, writers from different historical periods imagine, for instance, the problem of growing up female in very different ways. If teachers locate subcategories within our major thematic lists, they can ask students to deal with the historical evolution of attitudes toward such crucial matters: focusing on women's education, for example, students might compare Mary Astell's justification for and vision of a female institution of higher learning with Woolf's writing on a women's college. In addition, students might consider women's responses to specific historic events. Analyzing the impact of the Second World War, for example, they could study the work of Edith Sitwell, Elizabeth Bowen, Kay Boyle, and Muriel Rukeyser, to determine whether or not these artists shared a particular vocabulary of protest. Similarly, both the lesbian and the black traditions would be illuminated by comparing earlier writers with later authors who are in some sense revising their precursors' assumptions. The list of questions that follows is meant to suggest some useful approaches to thematically organized essay questions and research topics.

1. Students interested in a particular theme might wish to construct a fictional dialogue between two writers who deal with the same subject. What would Mary Wollstonecraft have to say to Adrienne Rich, and vice versa? Would Amelia Lanier, Christina Rossetti, Stevie Smith, Judith Wright, and Dorothy Livesay agree or disagree about the biblical figure of Eve?
2. It might be useful to ask students to consider why the assumptions about gender in different historical periods led women writers to approach a common theme in very different ways. The feminist work of Astell, Montagu, and Wollstonecraft, for example, could be compared to nineteenth-century feminist polemics or contemporary feminist argumentation. Similarly, it might be interesting to contrast the visions of female

divinity in Julian of Norwich's _Showings_ with
Jane Lead's and H.D.'s celebrations of figures
who seem to function as goddesses.

3. Listed under the thematic table "Death"
there are a number of texts dealing with suicide,
just as there are several works listed under the
thematic table "Father-Daughter Relationships"
that focus on incest. Students could write about
the significance of suicide from _The Awakening_ to
"To Room 19" and the poetry of Parker, Rukeyser,
Plath, Sexton, and Jong. Similarly, they could
write about father-daughter incest in Mourning
Dove's "Coyote Takes His Daughter as a Wife,"
Sylvia Plath's "Daddy," and Toni Morrison's _The
Bluest Eye_.

4. Rather than asking students to deal with
a large issue like women's relationship to nature, teachers may want them to analyze women
poets' uses of, say, animal imagery. Emily Dickinson's spiders and worms, Marianne Moore's
snails and dragons, Elizabeth Bishop's roosters,
fish, and moose, and Sylvia Plath's bees--all
these iconic creatures could become the bases of
interesting papers and, taken together, they
might constitute a kind of female bestiary.

5. As gardeners, cooks, and preservers,
women have always had a special relationship to
food. Students might approach female culture
through the theme of food by focusing on fictional dinner parties or poetic images of culinary sorcery. More generally, they might investigate texts depicting anorexia (e.g., Glück's
"Dedication to Hunger").

6. Women's attitudes toward their bodies
surface in a number of texts in _NALW_--on abortion
(Brooks's "The Mother"), masturbation (Adcock's
"Against Coupling"), the onset of puberty (Morrison's _The Bluest Eye_ or McCarthy's "Names"),
prostitution (Margaret Walker's "Whores"), and
rape (Atwood's "Rape Fantasies"). Students could
be asked to find imaginative or theoretical works
inside or outside the anthology that further
illuminate some of these issues.

7. In "Cassandra," Nightingale claims that
"the next Christ will be a female Christ." To
what extent do parables of female sacrifice
(Schreiner's "A Little African Story" or Jackson's "The Lottery") use this same idea and why?

8. Studying the relationship between white

Americans and native Americans as depicted in
texts ranging from Mary Rowlandson's captivity
narrative to Mourning Dove's fables of origin to
Margaret Laurence's and Leslie Marmon Silko's
stories, students may want to look at further
works by native American women.  They might, for
example, read Ruth Underhill's transcription and
translation of Maria Chona's stories about her
growth and development within the Papago tribe in
the Southwest at the turn of the century, or--
among more recent works--they might look at writings by such women as Paula Gunn Allen and Wendy
Rose.  Similarly, students who wish to study the
image of the Jewish woman in literature could
compare texts by such writers as Yezierska,
Rukeyser, Olsen, and Paley to explore the ways in
which each defines the situation of the Jew in
the twentieth century.
   9.  Especially in the nineteenth century, a
number of writers claimed that there was a parallel between racism and sexism.  Interested students might investigate the ways in which this
connection has been defined and sustained;  they
might also wish to write essays evaluating its
validity.
   10.  In much women's fiction, the single
woman is often seen as quite poor and emotionally
deprived.  Teachers might ask students to analyze
the feminization of poverty, as it is presented
in literature from <u>Cranford</u> to "The Daughters of
the Late Colonel."
   11.  The complex relationship between
mothers and daughters can be related to what
several recent critics call "matrophobia" (fear
of becoming one's mother) or what we might call
"matrophilia" (desire for one's mother).  Using
the thematic tables on "Having a Mother" or
"Motherhood," teachers might direct students to a
number of texts in <u>NALW</u> that analyze the source
of both these feelings, and ask them to write
papers on the interlocking phenomena of matrophobia and matrophilia.
   12. The figure of the witch and the powers
associated with sorcery or witchcraft have fasci-
nated women writers from Emily Dickinson to Mary
Elizabeth Coleridge, Marianne Moore, and Anne
Sexton.  Some students might wish to research the
historical reasons for the identification of
witchcraft with women or they might like to ex-

plore the images of witchcraft and sorcery in
women's literature.

13.   Throughout <u>NALW</u>, various occupations
continue to surface as central in women's lives
and letters:  in the nineteenth century, gover-
nessing and prostitution; in the twentieth century, domestic or white-collar work.  Students
might like to do background research on women's
participation in the work force or to examine the
literary presentation of various female-identi-
fied occupations.

14.   Because they are readers themselves,
students might wish to examine the ways in which
women writers have historically depicted female
reading habits.  From the polemics of Mary Wollstonecraft and the parodies of Jane Austen to the
confessions of Florence Nightingale, it is possible to trace a specifically female (and implicitly feminist) attack on the romance, which many
women of letters see as a destructive genre,
particularly for women readers.  Such a study
would be interesting in light of the stereotypical concepts of "women's fiction" that are still
operative in women's magazines and in, e.g.,
Harlequin Romances.

15.   Recent literary critical work on the
dynamics of a female literary matrilineage could
be used to engage students in the question of why
and how women writers invoke their predecessors
and contemporaries.  Many of the texts listed
under the thematic tables "Women on Specific
Women" and "Women and Creativity" would be pertinent to such an investigation.  Do female precursors function as enabling muse figures or disab-
ling inhibitors?

16. A number of stories in <u>NALW</u> analyze the
impact of male literary activity on women readers
and writers.  Students might want to compare the
depiction of a literary patrilineage in, say,
Wharton's "The Angel at the Grave" with the portrait of a literary father offered in Spark's
"The Fathers' Daughters."  Do contemporary efforts to recover a literary matrilineage (for
instance, in Sarton's "My Sisters, O My Sisters"
or Walker's "In Search of Our Mothers' Gardens")
solve the problem posed by these stories or does
the female literary tradition remain a puzzle for
contemporary women of letters?

## WOMEN'S STUDIES ISSUES

Almost all of the themes listed in this
manual represent subjects in women's history and
culture that have been addressed by women's
studies scholars.  Students interested in American working-class literature can read, for example, Rosalind Baxandall, Linda Gordon, and Susan
Reverby's America's Working Women;  students
studying English Victorian feminism can be sent
to Joseph Ambrose Banks's and Olive Banks's Feminism and Family Planning in Victorian England and
Martha Vicinus's anthologies, Suffer and Be Still
or The Widening Sphere;  students analyzing contemporary images of the female body can read the
Boston Woman's Collective's Our Bodies, Ourselves, Susan Brownmiller's Against Our Will:
Women, Men, and Rape, or Laura Lederer's collection of essays, Take Back the Night.  Because the
list of research questions related to women's
studies issues could be endless, those that follow only begin to suggest ways to link the material in NALW with interdisciplinary issues in
women's studies.

1.  Most of the periods covered by NALW have
been treated by feminist historians, especially
feminist historians of the American past.  Should
teachers wish to analyze the relationships between social history and literature in, for example, nineteenth- and twentieth-century America,
they could ask students to read such historical
texts as Catherine Clinton's The Other Civil War:
American Women in the Nineteenth Century or Susan
Ware's Holding Their Own: American Women in the
1930s. Students could base their research on a
particular issue in women's literature or on an
analysis of the relationship between social fact
and literary fiction.
2.  Women's studies students might be asked
to supplement their readings in NALW with an
investigation into the works of those authors who
had to be excluded because of space considerations, particularly when the writers in question
are central to the evolution of feminism.
Teachers can therefore ask students to compare
such turn-of-the-century activists as Olive
Schreiner and Charlotte Perkins Gilman with successors like Emma Goldman or Margaret Sanger.

Goldman's _Living My Life_ or Sanger's _Autobio-
graphy_ could be assigned, or students could be
directed to Linda Gordon's discussion of Goldman
and Sanger in _Woman's Body, Woman's Right_.  Similarly, students interested in English literary
history might want to supplement the selections
in _NALW_ with reading in the works of such feminists and modernists as Ray Strachey, Vera Brit-
tain, and Winifred Holtby.
    3. Students interested in the psychoanalytic
and sociocultural implications of motherhood
might choose some aspect of Adrienne Rich's examination of motherhood in _Of Woman Born_ or Nancy
Chodorow's analysis in _The Reproduction of
Mothering_ and compare such theoretical treatments
of maternity with the dramatizations of motherhood by some of the authors in _NALW_ who are
listed in our thematic tables on "Having a
Mother" and "Motherhood."
    4. Students might wish to relate women's
writings on general politics or on work to the
economic and sociological analyses of women's
status proposed by such works as Zillah Eisen-
stein's _Capitalist Patriarchy and the Case for
Socialist Feminism_ or Ann Oakley's _The Sociology
of Housework_.
    5.  Recent theorists of sexuality have begun
exploring the social construction of heterosexuality.  From Jean Baker Miller's _Towards a New
Psychology of Women_ to _Women:  Sex and Sexuality_,
edited by Catharine R. Stimpson and Ethel Spector
Person, such theorists analyze the nature and
evolution of female sexuality, and their explana-
tory models could be compared to the attitudes
toward eroticism that are implicitly dramatized
or explicitly articulated by a number of writers
in _NALW_ and listed in our thematic tables on
"Marriage," "Heterosexual Eroticism," and "Lesbianism."
    6.  Barbara Ehrenreich and Deirdre English
have written a short study entitled _Complaints
and Disorders_ about the sexual politics of sickness, a work that could be used as background for
the presentation of female sickness or invalidism
in such texts as Anne Finch's "The Spleen," Charlotte Brontë's _Jane Eyre_, Alice James's _Diary_,
and Charlotte Perkins Gilman's "The Yellow Wallpaper." More generally,  students could be asked
to do original research on the history of medical

attitudes toward women and the female body in any
given historical period, and then they could
relate their findings to the literature of that
period.

    7.  The history of psychological definitions
of deviance, from Kraft-Ebbing and Havelock Ellis
to Kinsey, could be used to contextualize lesbian
literary history.  In addition, the texts presented in NALW could be supplemented by consult-
ing Lesbian Studies, edited by Margaret Cruik-
shank, or Lillian Faderman's Surpassing the Love
of Men: Romantic Friendship and Love between
Women from the Renaissance to the Present.  Students could be asked to explore the relationship
between psychoanalytic theories about the nature
and origin of lesbianism in a given period and
lesbian writers' various presentations of themselves.

    8. Historians of the family like Carl Deg-
ler, William Chafe, Suzanne Steinmetz, and Murray
Strauss touch on subjects of importance to literary women:  divorce, child support laws, welfare,
alimony laws, sex education, domestic violence,
etc.   In addition, such anthologies as Women,
the Family, and Freedom, edited by Susan Groag
Bell and Karen Moffen, include important historical documents on the development of the family.
Using the tables on "The Family" in the fourth
section of this guide, teachers could ask students to consider the centrality in the female
literary tradition of any one of these topics.

    9.  To what extent do the images presented
in women's literature relate to the visual images
used in a given period by female painters?  Focusing on the Victorian period and the turn of
the century, students might compare representations of women in the art of Elizabeth Siddal,
Marie Spartali Stillman, and Mary Cassatt with
representations of women offered in texts by
Christina Rossetti, Olive Schreiner, and others;
in the modernist period, they could use images
produced by figures like Vanessa Bell or Dora
Carrington--or in the contemporary period, they
could use work by Georgia O'Keeffe, Miriam Sha-
piro, and Judy Chicago--to undertake similar
comparisons.  In all these cases, students might
want to consult essays by theorists and historians who analyze specific periods and styles of
female art:  both Old Mistresses: Women, Art,

and Ideology, by Rozsika Parker and Griselda
Pollock, and From the Center: Feminist Essays on
Women's Art, by Lucy Lippard, may be useful.
    10.  Sociological theories of sex role de-
velopment have proliferated since Margaret Mead
published Sex and Temperament. Students might
choose any one such theory and (using our thematic tables) test it against the literature about
growing up female in NALW.
    11.  From Carolyn Heilbrun's work on andro-
gyny to Robert Stoller's research into transsexu-
ualism and transvestism, investigators have envisioned or examined various alternatives to traditional sex roles. Students might be asked to
locate and analyze those texts in the anthology
that engage in comparable projects.
    12.  All of the ethnic writers in NALW could
be considered in terms of recent research on the
economic, social, and political situation of
minority women. Angela Davis's Women, Race and
Class, Bell Hooks's Ain't I a Woman: Black Women
and Feminism, and Claudia Tate's Black Women
Writers at Work might serve as background for
studies of the distinctive perspectives on society represented by the texts of black literary
women included in NALW; similarly,  Rayne
Greene's Native American Women: A Contextual
Bibliography could send students to supplementary
materials that would illuminate the contexts in
which the native American women writers whose
texts are included in NALW worked; finally, Charlotte Baum, Paula Hyman, and Sonya Michel's The
Jewish Woman in America and Elizabeth Koltun's
The Jewish Woman raise issues that might aid in
an understanding of the writings of Jewish women
included in NALW.
    13.  Students interested in the relation-
ships between religious studies and literary
history might begin their research by reading
Rosemary Ruether and Eleanor McLaughlin's Women
of Spirit: Female Leadership in the Jewish and
Christian Traditions. This survey of ascetic and
Quaker women, mystics, nuns, and reformers suggests the ways in which such authors as Julian of
Norwich and Jane Lead can be contextualized in
terms of the history of religion. Similarly,
students interested in revisionary mythologies
within Christianity might begin their research
with Elaine Pagels' The Gnostic Gospels.

14.   The parallels and discrepancies between literary women's writing on education and women's current situation in the academy could be dramatized for students on their own college and university campuses. _A Feminist Perspective on the Academy:  The Difference It Makes_, edited by Elizabeth Langland and Walter Gove, might help them understand the impact of feminism on various disciplines and inspire papers on the relationship between feminist visions of an ideal education (for instance, those described by Virginia Woolf in "A Woman's College from the Outside," _A Room of One's Own_, and _Three Guineas_) and the reality of women's education today.


MALE AND FEMALE LITERARY TRADITIONS

Once again, the subjects for analysis in this area are innumerable, for students could be asked to analyze the impact of gender on the dynamics of literary creativity, to pair individual authors, to compare male and female uses of particular genres, to contrast the contributions of men and women in a given period, or to explore questions related to periodization.

1.   Feminist scholars have identified and documented various images of women that emerge in male-authored literature.  Are there recurrent images of men in female-authored literature?  If so, are they stereotypical?  Are they misandric?
2.   Does a woman poet have a muse, and if so, what is his/her/its sex?  Traditionally, of course, the muse (for male poets) is female, a fact which might imply that (as Joanne Feit Diehl has argued in "Come Slowly--Eden:  The Woman Poet and Her Muse") the woman poet has a _male_ muse. _NALW_, however, includes poems which suggest that the woman poet may define the source of her creativity in terms of a range of possibilities: Dickinson's so-called "Master" letters and some of her poems about a male muse-figure, for instance, are balanced by H.D.'s depiction of a female muse-figure in _Trilogy_, by May Sarton's image of "The Muse as Medusa," and by Sylvia Plath's depiction of the female "Disquieting Muses."  Students interested in poetry and literary history might want to set some of these

works in the context of male-authored writings to
or about the muse in order to define the similarities and differences between male and female
visions of the imagination.

3.   Do men and women address different
audiences, or do they imagine their readerships
in gender-specific terms?  Almost any of the
texts in NALW might be compared with male-
authored texts in papers designed to analyze the
nature of the audiences that male and female
writers are addressing or constructing.  When
Charlotte Brontë has Jane Eyre address the
reader, for instance, is she imagining a different kind of reader from the person to whom
Thackeray "speaks" throughout Vanity Fair?  When
H.D. invokes a "you" in Trilogy is she invoking
the same sort of "you" to whom D. H. Lawrence
directs his remarks in, for example, such poems
as "Peach" and "Pomegranate"?

4.   Do male and female authors have different
relationships to language?  Many of the works we
have listed under the thematic category "Creativity" illuminate authorial attitudes towards invented or inherited language.  Comparing such
texts with male texts that theorize about language (for instance, Wordsworth's Preface to
Lyrical Ballads or Whitman's Preface to the 1855
Leaves of Grass), some students might want to
study the question of "female language."  Advanced undergraduates and graduate students might
even wish to enrich their research into this
matter with readings in recent French or Anglo-
American theory on the subject (i.e., Hélène
Cixous's "The Laugh of the Medusa," Dale Spender's Man Made Language, or Robin Lakoff's Language and Woman's Place).

5.   Analyses of texts by any of the male-
female "pairs" mentioned in Section 5 of this
manual might serve as the basis for interesting
comparison-contrast essays.  Among works by writers who were related to each other by blood or
friendship, for instance, some of Dorothy Wordsworth's journal entries (or indeed some of her
poems) could be compared to poems from William
Wordsworth's Lyrical Ballads; Mary Shelley's
Frankenstein could be paralleled with Percy Shelley's Prometheus Unbound; Elizabeth Barrett
Browning's dramatic monologues "The Runaway Slave
at Pilgrim's Point" and "Mother and Poet" could

be set against dramatic monologues by Robert Browning (and more ambitious students might even want to compare her <u>Aurora Leigh</u> to his <u>The Ring and the Book</u>); Christina Rossetti's "Goblin Market" could be read with Dante Gabriel Rossetti's "Jenny"; Lady Gregory's "Spreading the News" could be related to one of Yeats's or Synge's plays (Synge's <u>The Playboy of the Western World</u> might be a particularly apt text for comparison here); Mansfield's "The Daughters of the Late Colonel" could be set against Lawrence's "The Daughters of the Vicar" or his "The Horse Dealer's Daughter"; and so forth.

Similarly, comparison-contrast essays could be written about texts by writers who were not relatives or associates but were contemporaries. One or two of Emily Dickinson's poems about death (for instance, "I heard a fly buzz when I died" or "I felt a funeral in my brain") could be set against Whitman's "Out of the Cradle Endlessly Rocking" or his "Crossing Brooklyn Ferry"; Marianne Moore's "Poetry" could be analyzed in relation to Wallace Stevens' "The Idea of Order at Key West" or his "To a High-Toned Old Christian Woman"; Audre Lorde's "Coal" could be compared with one or two poems by Imamu Amiri Baraka or Ishmael Reed.

Finally, as suggested in Section 5, it is possible to pair works by writers who address common topics or work with comparable themes, and such pairings could function as the bases for interesting student essays.  Mary Wollstonecraft's analyses of the female situation in <u>A Vindication of the Rights of Woman</u> could be related to John Stuart Mill's vision of <u>The Subjection of Women</u>, for instance; Charlotte Brontë's depiction of the Byronic hero in <u>Jane Eyre</u> could be set against Lord Byron's delineation of the outlaw hero in <u>Childe Harold</u>; Kate Chopin's fantasies of female defiance and freedom in <u>The Awakening</u> could be related to Mark Twain's fantasies of male defiance and freedom in <u>Huckleberry Finn</u>; Toni Morrison's characterization of the difficulties of growing up black in <u>The Bluest Eye</u> could be compared to Ralph Ellison's vision of black culture in <u>Invisible Man</u>; Anne Sexton's "confessional" verse could be related to the "confessional" poetry of Robert Lowell, John Berryman, or DeWitt Snodgrass.

6.   To what extent do the images of women presented by male-authored literature reflect the reality of women's lives?  In addition, how might such images affect literary women?  In considering the first of these questions, students might be asked to research the similarities and differences  between, say, Chaucer's fictional Wife of Bath and such a "real-life" contemporary as Margery Kempe, or between a Shakespeare heroine like Rosalind in As You Like It or Olivia in Twelfth Night and an actual Renaissance lady like Mary Sidney Herbert.  In considering the second of these questions, students might examine the impact of Milton's images of Sin and Eve in Paradise Lost on literary women who set out to revise Biblical stories of the fall, or they might explore the effects of Pope's, Swift's, and Johnson's ambivalence toward women on such female contemporaries and descendants as Anne Finch, Maria Edgeworth, and Jane Austen.

7.   Choosing works by contemporary artists writing in similar modes, students might wish to compare male and female concepts of heroism with male and female notions about what Ellen Moers, in Literary Women, has called "heroinism."  Do the novels of, say, Charles Dickens and Charlotte Brontë offer different visions of ideal male and female characters?  Do the works of Virginia Woolf and James Joyce emphasize different values? Meditations on these questions could form the bases of strong term papers on such roughly contemporary major works as Jane Eyre and David Copperfield, Mrs. Dalloway and Ulysses.

8.   Do male and female writers represent the process of growing up as one that is different for boys and girls?  Is there a distinctively female version of the Bildungsroman whose pattern can be traced from, for instance, Jane Austen's Northanger Abbey through Charlotte Brontë's Jane Eyre to Edith Wharton's Summer and Toni Morrison's The Bluest Eye?  If so, how is this female Bildungsroman similar to, yet different from, such classic male-authored "development novels" as Great Expectations, A Portrait of the Artist as a Young Man, and Sons and Lovers?  Perhaps in conjunction with some reading of developmental psychology, speculations on these issues could lead to useful research projects and term papers.

9.   How does the gender of the artist effect

her or his choice of genre?  Students of poetry
might wish to consider why women have not written
traditional epics or pastoral elegies, or they
might want to explain how and why women's use of,
for instance, the genre of the long poem has
transformed its conventions.  Comparisons of
female-authored dramatic monologues, narratives,
and sonnet-sequences (either based on the lists
offered earlier in this manual or drawn from
outside reading) with similar male-authored works
might inspire term papers with interesting insights into the effects of gender on genre.

      10.   Students of literary history might wish
to undertake research projects which allow them
to generalize about a given period.  How does the
accomplishment of women writers in, say, nineteenth-century America compare with the achieve-
ment of male writers?  Were the sexes establish-
ing two different traditions in this era?  From
Leslie Fiedler to Ann Douglas, scholars who work
with nineteenth-century American literature have
argued that the commercial success of women's
domestic or "sentimental" fiction led male artists to try to distance themselves and their
heroes from what Douglas calls "the feminization"
of culture.  Could comparable claims be made
about male and female traditions in the eighteenth-century or the modernist period?  Though
these are large issues, students could begin to
investigate them by reading a selected group of
female-authored texts--for instance, for those
interested in nineteenth-century America, Susan
Warner's <u>Wide</u> <u>Wide</u> <u>World</u>, Harriet Beecher Stowe's
<u>Uncle</u> <u>Tom's</u> <u>Cabin</u>, Maria Cummins's <u>The</u> <u>Lamp-</u>
<u>lighter</u>--in conjunction with male-authored texts
which appear to resist female or feminist
values--for instance, Hawthorne's <u>The</u> <u>Blithedale</u>
<u>Romance</u>, Melville's <u>Moby-Dick</u>, Twain's <u>Huckle-</u>
<u>berry</u> <u>Finn</u>--and then writing papers which attempt
to "place" those works in appropriate traditions.

      11.   How has women's literature shaped <u>male</u>
literature?  To what extent have male writers
participated in the construction of feminist
theory?  In what ways have they resisted, rejec-
ted, or parodied women's works and goals?  Students interested in these questions could produce
a series of lively research papers:  some might
wish to study the line of male feminists that
descends from John Stuart Mill (in England) and

Thomas Wentworth Higginson (in America) to George
Bernard Shaw (in England) and Henry Adams (in
America); others might wish to study the attacks
on, and parodies of, women's writing produced by
artists from Alexander Pope (in Three Hours after
Marriage) to Bret Harte (in "Miss Mix, by Ch-l-
tte Bront-") and Ernest Hemingway (in "The Lady
Poets with Footnotes").  In addition, some might
wish, more generally, to consider the ways in
which female literary innovations have affected
male writing:  good papers could be written, for
instance, on the way in which Charlotte Brontë's
production of a quasi-autobiography in Jane Eyre
influenced Dickens' production of a similar
quasi-autobiography in David Copperfield, or on
the way in which Dorothy Richardson's experimentation with "stream of consciousness" may have
influenced a range of male contemporaries, from
Joyce to Lawrence.  Finally, students interested
in researching male and female biographies might
like to investigate the relationship between male
art and female patronage:  papers could be written, for example, on the effect such a Renaissance aristocrat as Mary Sidney Herbert had on
the artists she befriended, or on the patron-
protégé relationships between Lady Gregory and
Yeats, May Sinclair and T. S. Eliot, Gertrude
Stein and Ernest Hemingway.

        12.  Advanced students interested in liter-
ary theory and in the processes of literary history might want to write papers examining the
different ways in which male and female writers
have experienced the psychodynamics of aesthetic
influence.  Beginning with the accounts of artis-
tic inheritance and self-definition offered by
such recent thinkers as Harold Bloom (in The
Anxiety of Influence and elsewhere) and Walter
Jackson Bate (in The Burden of the Past), these
students might trace the divergent ways in which
individual male and female artists defined their
literary "ancestries":  Virginia Woolf's vision
of a female tradition in which "we think back
through our mothers" could be compared, for instance, to the "silence, exile and cunning" of
which Joyce's Stephen Dedalus dreams, or Walt
Whitman's sense of oppression by a European tradition that lingered like a "corpse" in the house
of American literature could be contrasted with
Elizabeth Barrett Browning's wistful confession

that "I look everywhere for grandmothers and find none."

## ADDITIONAL SUGGESTIONS

Advanced graduate students might be interested in undertaking a number of bibliographical, biographical, and editorial projects which have yet to be approached by feminist scholars. As many of the headnotes in _NALW_ indicate, a great deal of work still needs to be done so that women's literary history can be properly documented. At present, for example, there are no definitive, modern, annotated editions of the works of such major writers as Anne Finch and Elizabeth Barrett Browning; in addition, many texts--for instance, works by Margaret Cavendish, Jane Lead, Amelia Lanier, Mary Sidney Herbert, and Mary Astell--are unavailable in _any_ edition (except for occasional volumes in rare book rooms); finally, critical biographies of some writers--for example, Lanier, Astell, Anzia Yezierska, Anna Wickham, and Muriel Rukeyser--have yet to appear. Such research projects could easily form the bases of doctoral dissertations, master's theses, and in some cases senior honors theses.